Highlights of Women's Earnings in 2011

U.S. Department of Labor
U.S. Bureau of Labor Statistics
October 2012

Report 1038

Highlights of Women's Earnings in 2011

U.S. Department of Labor
U.S. Bureau of Labor Statistics
October 2012

Report 1038

Introduction

In 2011, women who were full-time wage and salary workers had median usual weekly earnings of $684, about 82 percent of median earnings for male full-time wage and salary workers ($832). In 1979, the first year for which comparable earnings data are available, women earned 62 percent of what men earned. (See chart 1 and tables 1 and 13.)

This report presents earnings data from the Current Population Survey (CPS), a national monthly survey of approximately 60,000 households conducted by the U.S. Census Bureau for the U.S. Bureau of Labor Statistics (BLS). Information on earnings is collected from one-fourth of the CPS sample each month. Readers should note that the comparisons of earnings in this report are on a broad level and do not control for many factors that can be significant in explaining earnings differences. For a detailed description of the source of the data and an explanation of the concepts and definitions used, see the accompanying technical note.

Highlights

Full-time workers

- Median weekly earnings were highest for women age 35 to 64 in 2011, with little difference in the earnings of 35- to 44-year-olds ($734), 45- to 54-year-olds ($744), and 55- to 64-year-olds ($749). Among men, those age 45 to 64 had the highest earnings, with 45- to 54-year-olds ($979) having made about the same as 55- to 64-year-olds ($997). Young women and men age 16 to 24 had the lowest earnings ($421 and $455, respectively). (See table 1.)

- Among the age groupings of those 35 years and older, women had earnings that ranged from 75 percent to 81 percent of those of their male counterparts. Among younger workers, the earnings differences between women and men were not as great. Women earned 92 percent of what men earned among workers 25 to 34 years old and 93 percent as much as men among 16- to 24-year-olds. (See table 1.)

- Between 1979 and 2011, women's-to-men's earnings ratios rose for most age groups. Among 25- to 34-year-olds, for example, the ratio grew from 68 percent in 1979 to 92 percent in 2011, and the ratio for 45- to 54-year-olds increased from 57 percent to 76 percent. (See table 13.)

- Asian women and men earned more than their White, Black, and Hispanic or Latino counterparts in 2011. Among women, Whites ($703) earned 94 percent as much as Asians ($751), while Blacks ($595) and Hispanics ($518) earned 79 percent and 69 percent as much, respectively. In comparison, White men ($856) earned 88 percent as much as Asian men ($970); Black men ($653) earned 67 percent as much; and Hispanic men ($571), 59 percent. (See chart 2 and table 1.)

- Earnings differences between women and men were widest for Whites and for Asians. White women earned 82 percent as much as their male counterparts in 2011, while Asian women earned 77 percent as much as their male counterparts. In comparison, both Black and Hispanic women had median earnings that were 91 percent of those of their male counterparts. (See table 1.)

- Across the major race and Hispanic ethnicity categories, women's inflation-adjusted, or constant-dollar, earnings have risen significantly since 1979. Earnings growth has been sharpest for White women, outpacing that of their Black and Hispanic counterparts. Between 1979 and 2011, inflation-adjusted earnings for White women rose by 32 percent, compared with an increase of 22 percent for Black women and 14 percent for Hispanic women. In contrast, earnings for White and Black men in 2011 were about the same as in 1979, after adjusting for inflation, while Hispanic men's earnings were down by 10 percent from their 1979 constant-dollar level. (See table 19.) Asians were not included in this analysis because comparable data are not available back to 1979. (See note in table 19.)

- Median weekly earnings vary significantly by level of educational attainment. Among both women and

1

men age 25 and older, the weekly earnings of those without a high school diploma ($395 for women and $488 for men) were about two-fifths of those with a bachelor's degree or higher ($998 for women and $1,332 for men) in 2011. Women and men with a high school diploma who had not attended college earned a little more than half of what women and men with a bachelor's degree or higher did, and those with some college or an associate's degree earned around two-thirds as much. (See tables 1 and 6.)

- At each level of education, women have fared better than men with respect to earnings growth. Although both women and men without a high school diploma have experienced declines in inflation-adjusted earnings since 1979, the drop for women was significantly less than that for men: a 10-percent decrease for women—as opposed to a 33-percent decline for men. On an inflation-adjusted basis, earnings for women with a college degree have increased by 31 percent since 1979, while those of male college graduates have risen by 16 percent. (Data pertain to workers age 25 and older.) (See chart 3 and table 20.)

- Women working full time in management, business, and financial operations jobs had median weekly earnings of $977 in 2011, which is more than women earned in any other major occupational category. Within management, business, and financial operations occupations, women who were chief executives and computer and information systems managers had the highest median weekly earnings ($1,464 and $1,543, respectively). The second highest paying job group for women was professional and related occupations, in which their median weekly earnings were $919. Within professional and related occupations, women who were lawyers ($1,631), pharmacists ($1,898), and physicians ($1,527) had the highest earnings. (See table 2.)

- The occupational distributions of female and male full-time workers differ significantly. Compared with men, relatively few women work in construction, production, or transportation occupations, and women are far more concentrated in administrative support jobs. (See chart 4 and table 2.)

- Women are more likely than men to work in professional and related occupations. Within this occupational category, though, the proportion of women employed in the higher paying job groups is much smaller than the proportion of men employed in them. In 2011, 8 percent of female professionals were employed in the relatively high-paying computer and engineering fields, compared with 44 percent of male professionals. Professional women were more likely to work in education and healthcare occupations, in which the pay is generally lower than that for computer and engineering jobs. Sixty-nine percent of female professionals worked in the education and healthcare fields in 2011, compared with 30 percent of male professionals. (See table 2.)

- Of the 44.5 million women working full time in wage and salary jobs in 2011, a little more than one-third were mothers of children under age 18. Median weekly earnings for mothers of children under age 18 were $669. Earnings for women without children under 18 were $692. (See table 8.)

- Median weekly earnings and women's-to-men's earnings ratios vary by state of residence. The differences among the states reflect, in part, variation in the occupations and industries found in each state and in the age composition of each state's labor force. In general, the sampling error for the state estimates is considerably larger than it is for the national estimates; thus, comparisons of state estimates should be made with caution. (See table 3.)

- Among full-time workers (that is, those working 35 hours or more per week in a job), men are more likely than women to have a longer workweek. Twenty-five percent of men, compared with 14 percent of women, worked 41 or more hours per week, in 2011. Women were more likely than men to work 35 to 39 hours per week: 13 percent as opposed to 5 percent. A large majority of both male and female full-time workers had a 40-hour workweek; among these workers, women earned 88 percent as much as men earned. (Persons who usually work 35 or more hours per week but whose hours vary were excluded from this analysis.) (See table 5.)

Part-time workers

- Women are more likely than men to work part time—that is, less than 35 hours per week on a sole, or principal, job. Women who worked part time made up 26 percent of all female wage and salary workers in 2011. In contrast, 13 percent of men in wage and salary jobs worked part time. (See tables 4 and 5.)

- Unlike full-time workers, women and men who worked part time had similar median earnings. Median weekly earnings for female part-timers were $235 in 2011, little different than the $226 median for their male counterparts.

- Among part-time workers, men tend to be younger than women. Forty-three percent of male part-time workers were 16 to 24 years old, compared with 28 percent of female part-time workers in 2011. (See table 4.)

Workers paid by the hour

- Sixty-two percent of women and 56 percent of men employed in wage and salary jobs were paid by the hour in 2011. Women who were paid hourly rates had median hourly earnings of $11.98, 87 percent of the median for men paid by the hour ($13.80). (See tables 9, 10, 16, and 17.)

- In 2011, among workers who were paid hourly rates, 6 percent of women and 4 percent of men had hourly earnings at or below the prevailing federal minimum wage of $7.25. (See tables 11 and 12.)

- Among both women and men, hourly paid workers age 16 to 19 were the most likely to have earnings at or below the minimum wage. Twenty-three percent of teenage workers paid hourly rates earned the prevailing federal minimum wage or less in 2011, compared with just 3 percent of hourly paid workers age 25 and older. Among 20- to 24-year-olds, 10 percent had earnings at or below the minimum wage. (See table 11.)

Charts, Statistical Tables, and Technical Note

Chart 1. Women's earnings as a percent of men's, full-time wage and salary workers, 1979–2011 annual averages

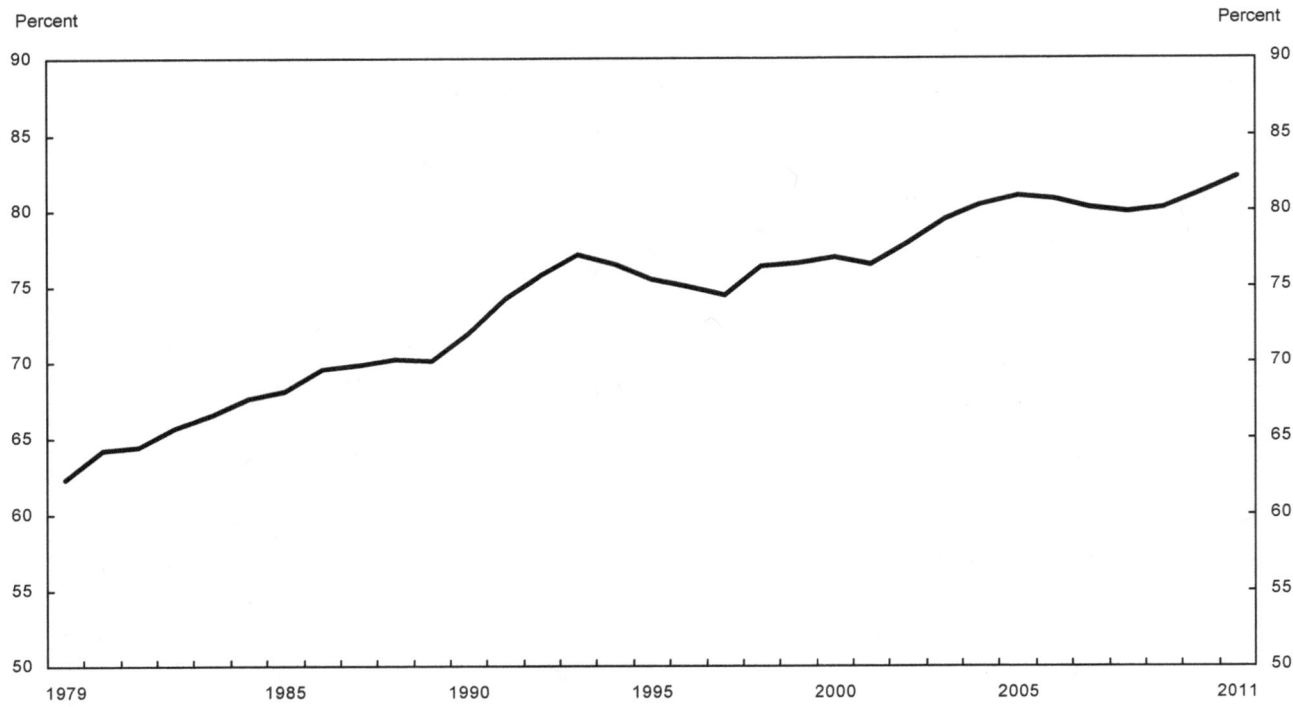

NOTE: Data relate to median usual weekly earnings of full-time wage and salary workers.
SOURCE: U.S. Bureau of Labor Statistics.

Chart 2. Median usual weekly earnings of full-time wage and salary workers by sex, race, and Hispanic or Latino ethnicity, 2011 annual averages

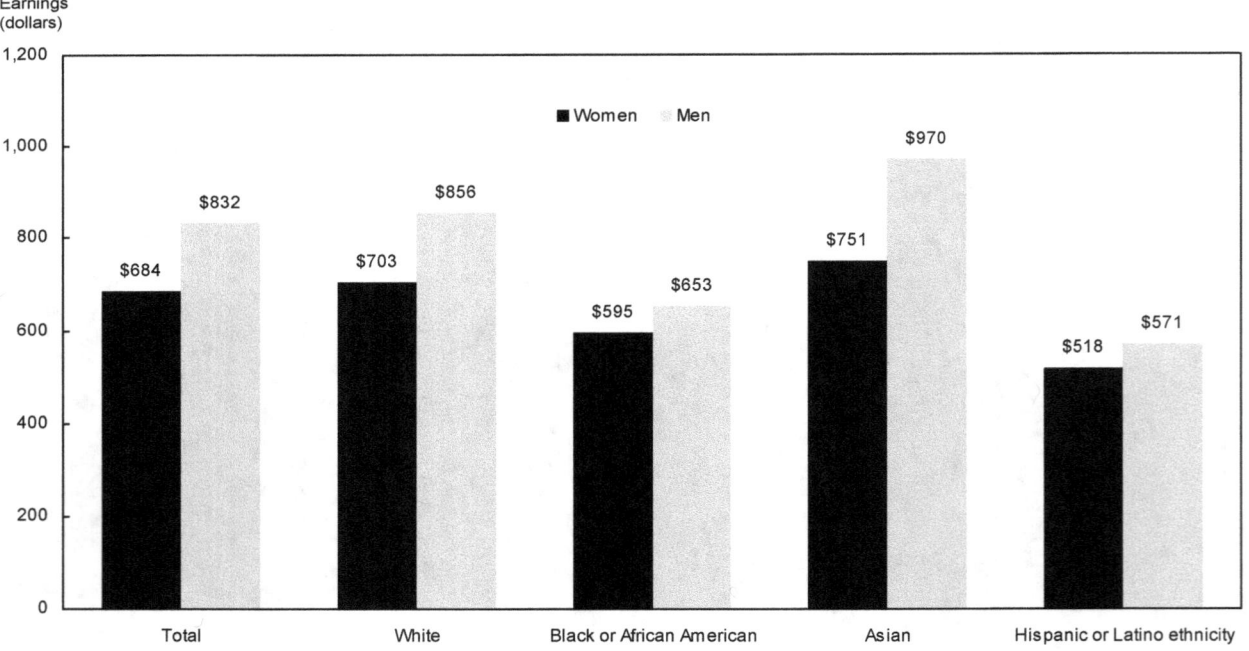

NOTE: Persons whose ethnicity is identified as Hispanic or Latino may be of any race.
SOURCE: U.S. Bureau of Labor Statistics.

Chart 3. Percent change in constant-dollar median usual weekly earnings, by educational attainment and sex, 1979–2011

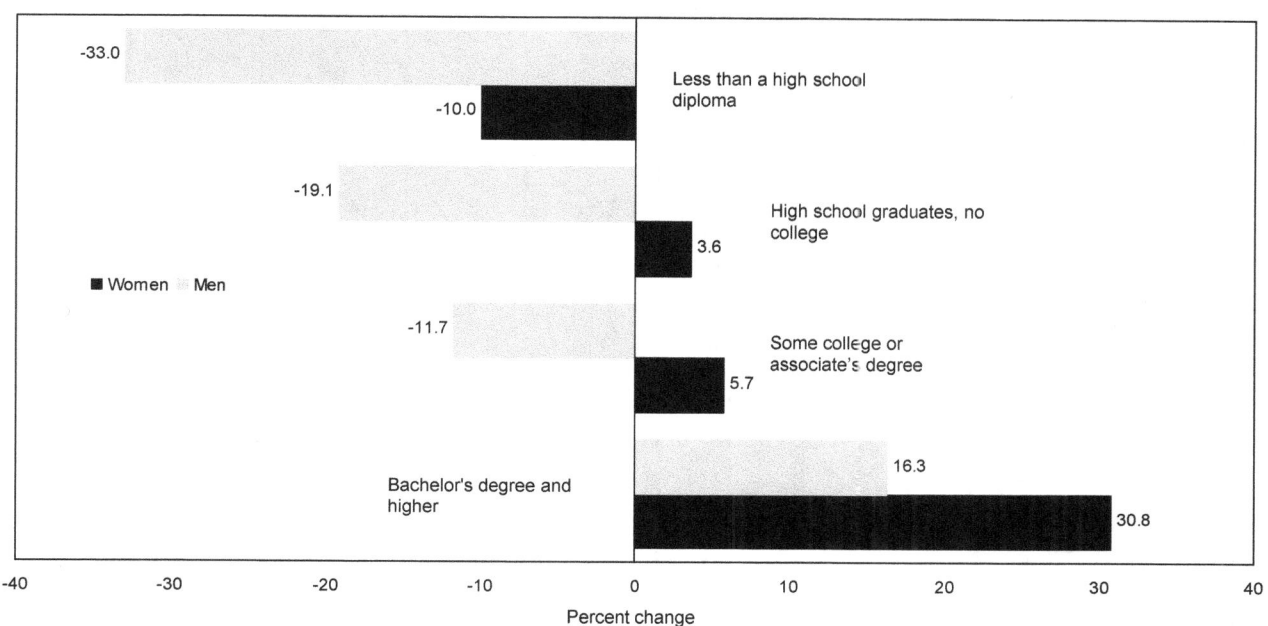

NOTE: Data relate to earnings of full-time wage and salary workers 25 years and older.
SOURCE: U.S. Bureau of Labor Statistics.

Chart 4. Distribution of full-time wage and salary employment, by sex and major occupation group, 2011 annual averages
Percent of total

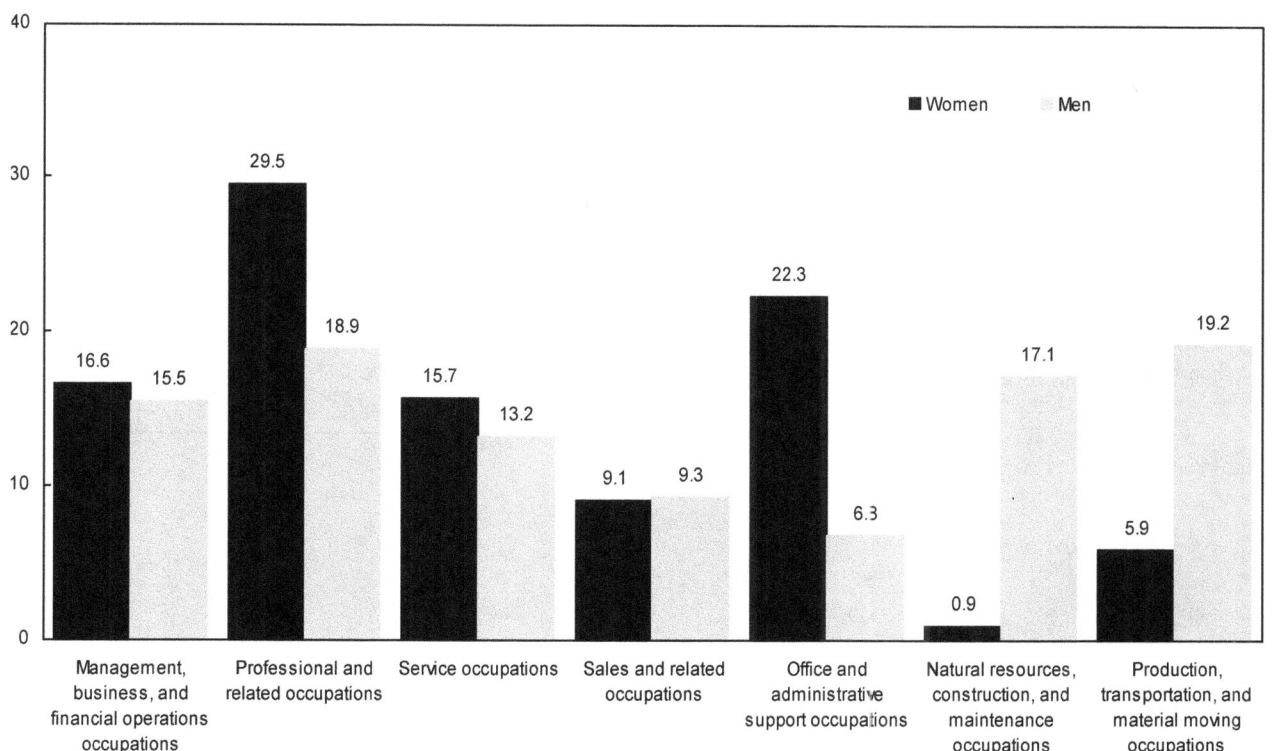

SOURCE: U.S. Bureau of Labor Statistics.

Table 1. Median usual weekly earnings of full-time wage and salary workers, by selected characteristics, 2011 annual averages

Characteristic	Both sexes			Women		
	Number of workers (in thousands)	Median weekly earnings	Standard error of median	Number of workers (in thousands)	Median weekly earnings	Standard error of median
Age						
Total, 16 years and older....................................	100,457	$756	$2	44,486	$684	$3
16 to 24 years...	8,723	440	4	3,772	421	3
16 to 19 years...	947	352	5	389	328	8
20 to 24 years...	7,776	457	4	3,383	438	5
25 years and older......................................	91,733	797	2	40,714	718	3
25 to 34 years...	24,296	693	3	10,392	662	5
35 to 44 years...	23,782	837	5	10,204	734	5
45 to 54 years...	25,133	866	5	11,557	744	5
55 to 64 years...	15,641	881	6	7,294	749	6
65 years and older....................................	2,881	742	10	1,266	664	14
Race and Hispanic or Latino Ethnicity						
White...	81,336	775	2	34,976	703	3
Black or African American.............................	11,604	615	3	6,191	595	4
Asian...	5,197	866	13	2,284	751	12
Hispanic or Latino ethnicity.............................	15,147	549	5	5,700	518	4
Marital Status						
Never married..	26,487	606	2	11,553	595	3
Married, spouse present...............................	57,050	858	3	23,274	741	3
Other marital status.....................................	16,920	722	4	9,660	662	5
Divorced..	11,374	758	5	6,461	697	7
Separated..	3,921	615	6	1,969	579	9
Widowed..	1,625	672	14	1,230	635	14
Union Affiliation[1]						
Members of unions[2]......................................	13,177	938	5	5,671	879	8
Represented by unions[3].................................	14,487	934	5	6,327	871	7
Not represented by a union.............................	85,969	729	2	38,159	653	3
Educational Attainment						
Total, 25 years and older................................	91,733	797	2	40,714	718	3
Less than a high school diploma......................	7,019	451	4	2,225	395	4
High school graduates, no college..................	25,157	638	3	10,220	554	4
Some college or associate's degree................	25,205	739	3	12,048	645	4
Bachelor's degree and higher.........................	34,353	1,150	3	16,221	998	5

See footnotes at end of table.

Characteristic	Mer			Women's earnings as a percent of men's
	Number of workers (in thousands)	Median weekly earnings	Standard error of median	
Age				
Total, 16 years and older....................................	55,971	$852	$3	82.2
16 to 24 years..	4,951	455	5	92.5
16 to 19 years...	558	370	7	88.6
20 to 24 years...	4,393	470	5	93.2
25 years and older...	51,020	886	3	81.0
25 to 34 years...	13,905	717	5	92.3
35 to 44 years...	13,578	935	7	78.5
45 to 54 years...	13,576	979	6	76.0
55 to 64 years...	8,347	997	8	75.1
65 years and older.......................................	1,614	821	21	80.9
Race and Hispanic or Latino Ethnicity				
White..	46,360	856	4	82.1
Black or African American................................	5,414	653	8	91.1
Asian..	2,912	970	15	77.4
Hispanic or Latino ethnicity.............................	9,448	571	5	90.7
Marital Status				
Never married...	14,934	614	3	96.9
Married, spouse present.................................	33,777	955	4	77.6
Other marital status.......................................	7,260	804	8	82.3
Divorced..	4,912	849	10	82.1
Separated...	1,953	670	15	86.4
Widowed..	395	843	48	75.3
Union Affiliation[1]				
Members of unions[2].......................................	7,506	982	7	89.5
Represented by unions[3].................................	8,160	981	6	88.8
Not represented by a union..............................	47,811	798	4	81.8
Educational Attainment				
Total, 25 years and older.................................	51,020	883	3	81.0
Less than a high school diploma.....................	4,794	483	3	80.9
High school graduates, no college...................	14,937	720	4	76.9
Some college or associate's degree.................	13,156	840	6	76.8
Bachelor's degree and higher..........................	18,132	1,332	8	74.9

[1] Differences in earnings levels between workers with and without union affiliation reflect a variety of factors in addition to coverage by a collective bargaining agreement, including the distribution of male and female employees by occupation, industry, firm size, and geographic region.

[2] Data refer to members of a labor union or an employee association similar to a union.

[3] Data refer to workers who report no union affiliation but whose jobs are covered by a union or an employee association contract, as well as to members of a labor union or an employee association similar to a union.

NOTE: Estimates for the race groups listed (White, Black or African American, and Asian) do not sum to totals because data are not presented for all races. Persons whose ethnicity is identified as Hispanic or Latino may be of any race.

SOURCE: U.S. Bureau of Labor Statistics.

Table 2. Median usual weekly earnings of full-time wage and salary workers, by detailed occupation and sex, 2011 annual averages

Occupation	Both sexes			Women		
	Number of workers (in thousands)	Median weekly earnings	Standard error of median	Number of workers (in thousands)	Median weekly earnings	Standard error of median
Total, 16 years and older...............................	100,457	$756	$2	44,486	$684	$3
Management, professional, and related occupations......	39,791	1,082	5	20,524	941	3
Management, business, and financial operations occupations....................................	16,061	1,160	5	7,386	977	7
Management occupations................................	10,891	1,237	9	4,440	1,018	11
Chief executives.......................................	990	1,963	62	245	1,464	69
General and operations managers....................	921	1,191	44	270	972	32
Legislators..	13	–	–	4	–	–
Advertising and promotions managers...............	68	1,164	26	40	–	–
Marketing and sales managers.......................	891	1,408	37	392	1,127	47
Public relations and fundraising managers...........	62	1,475	146	29	–	–
Administrative services managers...................	115	1,021	97	44	–	–
Computer and information systems managers......	530	1,579	52	138	1,543	76
Financial managers....................................	1,044	1,166	18	567	991	25
Compensation and benefits managers...............	21	–	–	14	–	–
Human resources managers..........................	207	1,331	58	149	1,273	83
Training and development managers.................	36	–	–	12	–	–
Industrial production managers.......................	250	1,211	48	45	–	–
Purchasing managers..................................	183	1,242	51	89	1,026	56
Transportation, storage, and distribution managers.................................	229	882	42	33	–	–
Farmers, ranchers, and other agricultural managers.................................	98	800	51	17	–	–
Construction managers................................	464	1,268	57	31	–	–
Education administrators..............................	735	1,228	36	467	1,061	38
Architectural and engineering managers............	98	1,914	38	7	–	–
Food service managers...............................	675	660	19	314	599	18
Funeral service managers............................	8	–	–	5	–	–
Gaming managers.....................................	22	–	–	7	–	–
Lodging managers.....................................	91	883	75	55	841	36
Medical and health services managers..............	450	1,252	37	325	1,166	46
Natural sciences managers...........................	12	–	–	7	–	–
Postmasters and mail superintendents..............	29	–	–	19	–	–
Property, real estate, and community association managers....................	317	921	27	182	728	29
Social and community service managers.............	277	1,045	44	196	973	35
Emergency management directors....................	5	–	–	1	–	–
Managers, all other...................................	2,050	1,265	27	737	1,047	48
Business and financial operations occupations........	5,170	1,038	10	2,946	937	8
Agents and business managers of artists, performers, and athletes....................	25	–	–	13	–	–
Buyers and purchasing agents, farm products......	7	–	–	2	–	–
Wholesale and retail buyers, except farm products...................................	130	882	38	62	849	34
Purchasing agents, except wholesale, retail, and farm products..	226	1,015	45	118	945	34
Claims adjusters, appraisers, examiners, and investigators...................................	271	913	41	162	804	41
Compliance officers...................................	176	1,125	58	78	995	35
Cost estimators..	106	1,080	104	19	–	–
Human resources workers............................	522	938	23	406	912	25
Compensation, benefits, and job analysis specialists...................................	53	893	250	39	–	–

See note at end of table.

Occupation	Men			Women's earnings as a percent of men's
	Number of workers (in thousands)	Median weekly earnings	Standard error of median	
Total, 16 years and older..	55,971	$832	$3	82.2
Management, professional, and related occupations......	19,267	¯,269	9	74.2
Management, business, and financial operations occupations....................................	8,676	¯,370	11	71.3
Management occupations................................	6,451	¯,427	14	71.3
Chief executives..	745	2,122	89	69.0
General and operations managers....................	651	1,319	65	73.7
Legislators..	9	–	–	–
Advertising and promotions managers...............	28	–	–	–
Marketing and sales managers......................	499	¯,660	35	67.9
Public relations and fundraising managers...........	33	–	–	–
Administrative services managers....................	71	¯,170	128	–
Computer and information systems managers......	392	1,595	63	96.7
Financial managers....................................	477	¯,504	49	65.9
Compensation and benefits managers...............	7	–	–	–
Human resources managers..........................	58	¯,488	98	85.6
Training and development managers.................	24	–	–	–
Industrial production managers........................	204	¯,245	44	–
Purchasing managers.................................	94	¯,368	70	75.0
Transportation, storage, and distribution managers................................	196	861	40	–
Farmers, ranchers, and other agricultural managers................................	81	855	120	–
Construction managers.................................	433	¯,325	112	–
Education administrators...............................	268	¯,532	66	69.3
Architectural and engineering managers.............	91	¯,908	36	–
Food service managers................................	361	734	18	81.6
Funeral service managers.............................	4	–	–	–
Gaming managers......................................	15	–	–	–
Lodging managers......................................	36	–	–	–
Medical and health services managers..............	125	¯,456	53	80.1
Natural sciences managers...........................	5	–	–	–
Postmasters and mail superintendents...............	10	–	–	–
Property, real estate, and community association managers....................	135	1,201	95	60.6
Social and community service managers.............	81	1,221	165	79.7
Emergency management directors....................	4	–	–	–
Managers, all other....................................	1,313	1,406	28	74.5
Business and financial operations occupations........	2,225	1,225	22	76.5
Agents and business managers of artists, performers, and athletes....................	12	–	–	–
Buyers and purchasing agents, farm products......	5	–	–	–
Wholesale and retail buyers, except farm products....................................	68	928	49	91.5
Purchasing agents, except wholesale, retail, and farm products...	108	1,129	41	83.7
Claims adjusters, appraisers, examiners, and investigators......................................	110	1,077	59	74.7
Compliance officers....................................	98	1,279	227	77.8
Cost estimators..	87	1,117	89	–
Human resources workers............................	116	1,053	57	86.6
Compensation, benefits, and job analysis specialists....................................	13	–	–	–

See note at end of table.

Occupation	Both sexes			Women		
	Number of workers (in thousands)	Median weekly earnings	Standard error of median	Number of workers (in thousands)	Median weekly earnings	Standard error of median
Training and development specialists.............	117	$1,059	$144	64	$951	$57
Logisticians..........................	77	864	43	27	–	–
Management analysts............................	458	1,355	33	208	1,174	72
Meeting, convention, and event planners............	87	889	36	71	892	46
Fundraisers..............................	56	1,064	63	42	–	–
Market research analysts and marketing specialists...................	167	1,157	33	101	1,029	65
Business operations specialists, all other............	238	991	30	149	908	84
Accountants and auditors............................	1,383	1,056	17	852	956	13
Appraisers and assessors of real estate.............	50	990	45	20	–	–
Budget analysts........................	52	1,174	138	30	–	–
Credit analysts............................	21	–	–	12	–	–
Financial analysts........................	63	1,737	36	22	–	–
Personal financial advisors........................	270	1,239	47	97	941	31
Insurance underwriters........................	108	970	53	64	939	30
Financial examiners........................	7	–	–	5	–	–
Credit counselors and loan officers..................	306	1,024	40	159	829	33
Tax examiners and collectors, and revenue agents........................	67	920	51	40	–	–
Tax preparers....................	55	701	62	41	–	–
Financial specialists, all other........................	72	913	47	41	–	–
Professional and related occupations....................	23,730	1,029	5	13,139	919	5
Computer and mathematical occupations..............	3,296	1,305	26	787	1,126	23
Computer and information research scientists......	19	–	–	2	–	–
Computer systems analysts..........................	373	1,328	49	132	1,144	49
Information security analysts..........................	45	–	–	7	–	–
Computer programmers....................	411	1,277	65	83	1,238	29
Software developers, applications and systems software.........	990	1,558	24	179	1,388	41
Web developers....................	117	1,017	40	35	–	–
Computer support specialists........................	434	915	39	107	951	44
Database administrators....................	138	1,238	94	48	–	–
Network and computer systems administrators.....	221	1,180	46	49	–	–
Computer network architects........................	94	1,441	97	12	–	–
Computer occupations, all other....................	282	1,127	43	61	998	56
Actuaries........................	17	–	–	5	–	–
Mathematicians....................	2	–	–	1	–	–
Operations research analysts....................	116	1,273	87	51	1,326	213
Statisticians....................	30	–	–	13	–	–
Miscellaneous mathematical science occupations....................	6	–	–	2	–	–
Architecture and engineering occupations..............	2,494	1,315	20	316	1,140	28
Architects, except naval....................	113	1,325	149	21	–	–
Surveyors, cartographers, and photogrammetrists....................	31	–	–	5	–	–
Aerospace engineers....................	134	1,621	109	16	–	–
Agricultural engineers....................	1	–	–	–	–	–
Biomedical engineers....................	12	–	–	2	–	–
Chemical engineers....................	73	1,757	99	16	–	–
Civil engineers....................	335	1,398	50	46	–	–
Computer hardware engineers....................	76	1,528	66	10	–	–
Electrical and electronics engineers..................	283	1,442	36	26	–	–
Environmental engineers....................	36	–	–	10	–	–
Industrial engineers, including health and safety...	178	1,336	33	34	–	–

See note at end of table.

Table 2. Median usual weekly earnings of full-time wage and salary workers, by detailed occupation and sex, 2011 annual averages—cont'd

Occupation	Men			Women's earnings as a percent of men's
	Number of workers (in thousands)	Median weekly earnings	Standard error of median	
Training and development specialists.................	53	$1,260	$74	75.5
Logisticians..	50	938	34	–
Management analysts......................................	250	1,514	110	77.5
Meeting, convention and event planners.............	16	–	–	–
Fundraisers..	14	–	–	–
Market research analysts and marketing specialists..	66	1,446	69	71.2
Business operations specialists, all other...........	88	1,185	52	76.6
Accountants and auditors...............................	532	1,250	29	76.5
Appraisers and assessors of real estate.............	30	–	–	–
Budget analysts..	22	–	–	–
Credit analysts...	9	–	–	–
Financial analysts...	40	–	–	–
Personal financial advisors.............................	173	1,535	172	61.3
Insurance underwriters...................................	44	–	–	–
Financial examiners.......................................	2	–	–	–
Credit counselors and loan officers...................	147	1,345	35	61.6
Tax examiners and collectors, and revenue agents..	27	–	–	–
Tax preparers..	13	–	–	–
Financial specialists, all other.........................	30	–	–	–
Professional and related occupations.....................	10,592	1,211	10	75.9
Computer and mathematical occupations..............	2,509	1,369	17	82.2
Computer and information research scientists......	17	–	–	–
Computer systems analysts.............................	242	1,410	75	81.1
Information security analysts...........................	38	–	–	–
Computer programmers..................................	329	1,330	55	93.1
Software developers, applications and systems software...	812	1,606	43	86.4
Web developers..	81	1,033	42	–
Computer support specialists..........................	326	896	47	106.1
Database administrators.................................	90	1,470	83	–
Network and computer systems administrators.....	172	1,243	52	–
Computer network architects...........................	81	1,585	190	–
Computer occupations, all other......................	221	1,165	49	85.7
Actuaries..	12	–	–	–
Mathematicians..	1	–	–	–
Operations research analysts..........................	66	1,258	110	105.4
Statisticians..	17	–	–	–
Miscellaneous mathematical science occupations..	5	–	–	–
Architecture and engineering occupations..............	2,178	1,343	13	84.9
Architects, except naval.................................	92	1,351	39	–
Surveyors, cartographers, and photogrammetrists......................................	26	–	–	–
Aerospace engineers.....................................	119	1,745	54	–
Agricultural engineers....................................	1	–	–	–
Biomedical engineers.....................................	10	–	–	–
Chemical engineers.......................................	57	1,885	34	–
Civil engineers...	289	1,436	41	–
Computer hardware engineers.........................	66	1,546	34	–
Electrical and electronics engineers..................	256	1,455	34	–
Environmental engineers................................	26	–	–	–
Industrial engineers, including health and safety...	143	1,356	33	–

See note at end of table.

13

Occupation	Both sexes			Women		
	Number of workers (in thousands)	Median weekly earnings	Standard error of median	Number of workers (in thousands)	Median weekly earnings	Standard error of median
Marine engineers and naval architects	6	–	–	1	–	–
Materials engineers	30	–	–	4	–	–
Mechanical engineers	306	$1,374	$34	16	–	–
Mining and geological engineers, including mining safety engineers	9	–	–	1	–	–
Nuclear engineers	23	–	–	2	–	–
Petroleum engineers	19	–	–	1	–	–
Engineers, all other	310	1,366	29	35	–	–
Drafters	124	941	117	23	–	–
Engineering technicians, except drafters	341	954	32	40	–	–
Surveying and mapping technicians	53	777	100	6	–	–
Life, physical, and social science occupations	1,043	1,108	23	479	$1,038	$33
Agricultural and food scientists	27	–	–	10	–	–
Biological scientists	103	1,031	99	50	853	24
Conservation scientists and foresters	22	–	–	4	–	–
Medical scientists	141	1,109	61	78	1,127	110
Astronomers and physicists	18	–	–	4	–	–
Atmospheric and space scientists	7	–	–	1	–	–
Chemists and materials scientists	83	1,169	60	38	–	–
Environmental scientists and geoscientists	86	1,383	90	25	–	–
Physical scientists, all other	133	1,383	48	51	1,167	244
Economists	20	–	–	8	–	–
Survey researchers	1	–	–	–	–	–
Psychologists	104	1,229	63	74	1,244	59
Sociologists	2	–	–	2	–	–
Urban and regional planners	19	–	–	9	–	–
Miscellaneous social scientists and related workers	48	–	–	29	–	–
Agricultural and food science technicians	13	–	–	6	–	–
Biological technicians	19	–	–	9	–	–
Chemical technicians	69	788	79	29	–	–
Geological and petroleum technicians	6	–	–	3	–	–
Nuclear technicians	3	–	–	1	–	–
Social science research assistants	1	–	–	–	–	–
Miscellaneous life, physical, and social science technicians	118	763	35	49	–	–
Community and social services occupations	1,931	813	13	1,202	772	10
Counselors	568	828	24	380	808	27
Social workers	684	817	18	554	798	18
Probation officers and correctional treatment specialists	86	822	101	44	–	–
Social and human service assistants	105	597	46	83	597	58
Miscellaneous community and social service specialists, including health educators and community health workers	62	676	74	39	–	–
Clergy	343	945	28	51	889	93
Directors, religious activities and education	34	–	–	25	–	–
Religious workers, all other	50	654	81	26	–	–
Legal occupations	1,259	1,277	50	676	1,003	36
Lawyers	704	1,774	62	242	1,631	121
Judicial law clerks	4	–	–	3	–	–
Judges, magistrates, and other judicial workers	58	1,655	124	26	–	–
Paralegals and legal assistants	338	824	28	286	813	30
Miscellaneous legal support workers	155	815	28	120	788	23

See note at end of table.

Table 2. **Median usual weekly earnings of full-time wage and salary workers, by detailed occupation and sex, 2011 annual averages—cont'd**

Occupation	Men			Women's earnings as a percent of men's
	Number of workers (in thousands)	Median weekly earnings	Standard error of median	
Marine engineers and naval architects...............	6	–	–	–
Materials engineers.......................................	26	–	–	–
Mechanical engineers....................................	290	$1,399	$36	–
Mining and geological engineers, including mining safety engineers.............................	8	–	–	–
Nuclear engineers...	20	–	–	–
Petroleum engineers......................................	18	–	–	–
Engineers, all other......................................	275	1,361	28	–
Drafters...	102	1,052	128	–
Engineering technicians, except drafters.............	301	952	31	–
Surveying and mapping technicians..................	47	–	–	–
Life, physical, and social science occupations.........	565	1,156	30	89.8
Agricultural and food scientists........................	17	–	–	–
Biological scientists.......................................	53	1,177	73	72.5
Conservation scientists and foresters................	18	–	–	–
Medical scientists..	64	1,102	51	102.3
Astronomers and physicists.............................	15	–	–	–
Atmospheric and space scientists.....................	6	–	–	–
Chemists and materials scientists.....................	45	–	–	–
Environmental scientists and geoscientists..........	61	1,408	62	–
Physical scientists, all other...........................	82	1,483	101	78.7
Economists...	12	–	–	–
Survey researchers..	–	–	–	–
Psychologists...	31	–	–	–
Sociologists...	–	–	–	–
Urban and regional planners...........................	10	–	–	–
Miscellaneous social scientists and related workers...	19	–	–	–
Agricultural and food science technicians...........	7	–	–	–
Biological technicians....................................	10	–	–	–
Chemical technicians.....................................	40	–	–	–
Geological and petroleum technicians................	3	–	–	–
Nuclear technicians.......................................	2	–	–	–
Social science research assistants....................	1	–	–	–
Miscellaneous life, physical, and social science technicians..	69	807	107	–
Community and social services occupations...........	728	906	27	85.2
Counselors..	188	874	42	92.4
Social workers..	130	902	58	88.5
Probation officers and correctional treatment specialists..	41	–	–	–
Social and human service assistants	21	–	–	–
Miscellaneous community and social service specialists, including health educators and community health workers...........................	23	–	–	–
Clergy...	292	961	38	92.5
Directors, religious activities and education.........	10	–	–	–
Religious workers, all other.............................	24	–	–	–
Legal occupations..	583	1,758	30	57.1
Lawyers...	462	1,884	22	86.6
Judicial law clerks...	1	–	–	–
Judges, magistrates, and other judicial workers....	32	–	–	–
Paralegals and legal assistants........................	52	884	73	92.0
Miscellaneous legal support workers..................	35	–	–	–

See note at end of table.

Table 2. Median usual weekly earnings of full-time wage and salary workers, by detailed occupation and sex, 2011 annual averages—cont'd

Occupation	Both sexes			Women		
	Number of workers (in thousands)	Median weekly earnings	Standard error of median	Number of workers (in thousands)	Median weekly earnings	Standard error of median
Education, training, and library occupations............	6,518	$919	$7	4,769	$869	$7
Postsecondary teachers..................	925	1,209	34	399	1,093	61
Preschool and kindergarten teachers................	532	606	16	519	603	16
Elementary and middle school teachers.............	2,436	947	8	1,973	933	8
Secondary school teachers...........................	1,005	1,015	19	575	989	24
Special education teachers........................	364	939	19	308	935	19
Other teachers and instructors.....................	368	858	52	205	739	25
Archivists, curators, and museum technicians......	38	–	–	26	–	–
Librarians..........................	139	850	67	118	813	39
Library technicians........................	13	–	–	10	–	–
Teacher assistants..........................	605	480	15	566	471	13
Other education, training, and library workers......	94	982	75	71	979	87
Arts, design, entertainment, sports, and media occupations............	1,464	929	16	613	856	21
Artists and related workers.....................	56	1,115	107	21	–	–
Designers...........................	458	950	23	201	816	26
Actors....................	8	–	–	2	–	–
Producers and directors.....................	105	1,023	124	47	–	–
Athletes, coaches, umpires, and related workers...	109	825	59	25	–	–
Dancers and choreographers.....................	6	–	–	3	–	–
Musicians, singers, and related workers.............	35	–	–	5	–	–
Entertainers and performers, sports and related workers, all other.........................	7	–	–	4	–	–
Announcers..........................	32	–	–	9	–	–
News analysts, reporters and correspondents......	62	937	52	18	–	–
Public relations specialists.........................	123	954	46	75	887	51
Editors..........................	132	902	38	74	892	33
Technical writers..........................	46	–	–	26	–	–
Writers and authors..........................	85	918	36	43	–	–
Miscellaneous media and communication workers.	47	–	–	32	–	–
Broadcast and sound engineering technicians and radio operators........................	79	857	35	6	–	–
Photographers..........................	45	–	–	16	–	–
Television, video, and motion picture camera operators and editors........................	27	–	–	5	–	–
Media and communication equipment workers, all other..........................	2	–	–	1	–	–
Healthcare practitioner and technical occupations....	5,725	995	8	4,296	965	8
Chiropractors..........................	5	–	–	2	–	–
Dentists..........................	42	–	–	9	–	–
Dietitians and nutritionists........................	69	897	57	64	906	53
Optometrists..........................	9	–	–	3	–	–
Pharmacists..........................	195	1,917	28	110	1,898	29
Physicians and surgeons........................	573	1,860	104	206	1,527	92
Physician assistants........................	69	1,220	532	44	–	–
Podiatrists..........................	1	–	–	1	–	–
Audiologists..........................	14	–	–	10	–	–
Occupational therapists........................	72	1,189	47	62	1,193	58
Physical therapists..........................	146	1,322	70	87	1,216	102
Radiation therapists..........................	12	–	–	10	–	–
Recreational therapists..........................	10	–	–	7	–	–
Respiratory therapists..........................	126	997	44	73	1,028	56
Speech-language pathologists.....................	87	1,075	58	84	1,076	54
Exercise physiologists........................	2	–	–	1	–	–

See note at end of table.

Table 2. **Median usual weekly earnings of full-time wage and salary workers, by detailed occupation and sex, 2011 annual averages—cont'd**

Occupation	Men			Women's earnings as a percent of men's
	Number of workers (in thousands)	Median weekly earnings	Standard error of median	
Education, training, and library occupations............	1,749	$1,109	$22	78.4
Postsecondary teachers................................	526	1,358	37	80.5
Preschool and kindergarten teachers.................	13	–	–	–
Elementary and middle school teachers..............	463	1,022	21	91.3
Secondary school teachers............................	431	1,049	26	94.3
Special education teachers............................	55	967	67	96.7
Other teachers and instructors........................	163	1,105	61	66.9
Archivists, curators, and museum technicians......	12	–	–	–
Librarians..	21	–	–	–
Library technicians.....................................	3	–	–	–
Teacher assistants.....................................	39	–	–	–
Other education, training, and library workers.......	23	–	–	–
Arts, design, entertainment, sports, and media occupations..	850	995	29	86.0
Artists and related workers............................	36	–	–	–
Designers..	257	1,045	64	78.1
Actors..	6	–	–	–
Producers and directors...............................	58	1,130	473	–
Athletes, coaches, umpires, and related workers...	84	919	72	–
Dancers and choreographers..........................	3	–	–	–
Musicians, singers, and related workers.............	29	–	–	–
Entertainers and performers, sports and related workers, all other...................................	3	–	–	–
Announcers..	24	–	–	–
News analysts, reporters and correspondents......	44	–	–	–
Public relations specialists............................	49	–	–	–
Editors..	58	933	48	95.6
Technical writers..	20	–	–	–
Writers and authors....................................	42	–	–	–
Miscellaneous media and communication workers	15	–	–	–
Broadcast and sound engineering technicians and radio operators...................................	73	872	45	–
Photographers...	29	–	–	–
Television, video, and motion picture camera operators and editors...............................	22	–	–	–
Media and communication equipment workers, all other..	1	–	–	–
Healthcare practitioner and technical occupations....	1,429	1,129	23	85.5
Chiropractors..	3	–	–	–
Dentists..	33	–	–	–
Dietitians and nutritionists............................	6	–	–	–
Optometrists..	6	–	–	–
Pharmacists...	85	1,998	41	95.0
Physicians and surgeons..............................	366	1,935	114	78.9
Physician assistants...................................	24	–	–	–
Podiatrists...	–	–	–	–
Audiologists...	4	–	–	–
Occupational therapists................................	10	–	–	–
Physical therapists.....................................	59	1,522	106	79.9
Radiation therapists....................................	2	–	–	–
Recreational therapists.................................	3	–	–	–
Respiratory therapists..................................	53	966	52	106.4
Speech-language pathologists.........................	3	–	–	–
Exercise physiologists..................................	1	–	–	–

See note at end of table.

Occupation	Both sexes			Women		
	Number of workers (in thousands)	Median weekly earnings	Standard error of median	Number of workers (in thousands)	Median weekly earnings	Standard error of median
Therapists, all other...	83	$885	$42	64	$869	$86
Veterinarians..	40	–	–	28	–	–
Registered nurses...	2,145	1,039	19	1,937	1,034	18
Nurse anesthetists...	26	–	–	10	–	–
Nurse midwives..	2	–	–	2	–	–
Nurse practitioners...	81	1,461	44	69	1,432	39
Health diagnosing and treating practitioners, all other..	5	–	–	2	–	–
Clinical laboratory technologists and technicians...	282	861	39	206	845	49
Dental hygienists..	61	986	43	59	992	40
Diagnostic related technologists and technicians...	273	981	31	191	964	26
Emergency medical technicians and paramedics..	167	715	24	54	649	33
Health practitioner support technologists and technicians...	374	644	21	283	632	22
Licensed practical and licensed vocational nurses.	424	722	14	386	720	13
Medical records and health information technicians...	107	588	24	96	574	26
Opticians, dispensing......................................	34	–	–	26	–	–
Miscellaneous health technologists and technicians...	127	744	49	89	711	28
Other healthcare practitioners and technical occupations...	63	870	37	22	–	–
Service occupations..	14,378	486	2	6,991	433	4
Healthcare support occupations...........................	2,190	487	4	1,900	483	5
Nursing, psychiatric, and home health aides.........	1,305	453	7	1,134	446	7
Occupational therapy assistants and aides..........	12	–	–	11	–	–
Physical therapist assistants and aides...............	54	665	85	32	–	–
Massage therapists..	34	–	–	28	–	–
Dental assistants...	191	579	10	184	582	10
Medical assistants..	314	522	9	293	518	8
Medical transcriptionists..................................	44	–	–	43	–	–
Pharmacy aides...	23	–	–	14	–	–
Veterinary assistants and laboratory animal caretakers..	20	–	–	13	–	–
Phlebotomists...	94	521	21	77	516	19
Miscellaneous healthcare support occupations, including medical equipment preparers.............	98	487	25	72	480	27
Protective service occupations.............................	2,798	757	10	511	602	14
First-line supervisors of correctional officers........	41	–	–	11	–	–
First-line supervisors of police and detectives.......	101	1,083	148	18	–	–
First-line supervisors of fire fighting and prevention workers...	40	–	–	1	–	–
First-line supervisors of protective service workers, all other..	96	716	116	23	–	–
Firefighters...	291	1,000	29	11	–	–
Fire inspectors..	18	–	–	1	–	–
Bailiffs, correctional officers, and jailers..............	436	682	22	116	586	30
Detectives and criminal investigators..................	147	1,154	59	22	–	–
Fish and game wardens...................................	5	–	–	1	–	–
Parking enforcement workers.............................	5	–	–	2	–	–
Police and sheriff's patrol officers......................	653	947	22	75	938	61
Transit and railroad police................................	7	–	–	–	–	–
Animal control workers....................................	8	–	–	4	–	–
Private detectives and investigators....................	86	869	63	30	–	–

See note at end of table.

Table 2. **Median usual weekly earnings of full-time wage and salary workers, by detailed occupation and sex, 2011 annual averages—cont'd**

Occupation	Men			Women's earnings as a percent of men's
	Number of workers (in thousands)	Median weekly earnings	Standard error of median	
Therapists, all other..	19	–	–	–
Veterinarians..	12	–	–	–
Registered nurses..	208	$1,081	$44	95.7
Nurse anesthetists...	16	–	–	–
Nurse midwives..	–	–	–	–
Nurse practitioners...	11	–	–	–
Health diagnosing and treating practitioners, all other..	3	–	–	–
Clinical laboratory technologists and technicians...	77	888	45	95.2
Dental hygienists...	3	–	–	–
Diagnostic related technologists and technicians..	82	1,054	53	91.5
Emergency medical technicians and paramedics...	113	757	29	85.7
Health practitioner support technologists and technicians..	91	682	30	92.7
Licensed practical and licensed vocational nurses.	39	–	–	–
Medical records and health information technicians..	10	–	–	–
Opticians, dispensing......................................	8	–	–	–
Miscellaneous health technologists and technicians..	38	–	–	–
Other healthcare practitioners and technical occupations...	41	–	–	–
Service occupations...	7,387	551	7	78.6
Healthcare support occupations...........................	290	521	14	92.7
Nursing, psychiatric, and home health aides........	172	502	14	88.8
Occupational therapy assistants and aides..........	1	–	–	–
Physical therapist assistants and aides...............	22	–	–	–
Massage therapists..	6	–	–	–
Dental assistants...	7	–	–	–
Medical assistants..	21	–	–	–
Medical transcriptionists..................................	2	–	–	–
Pharmacy aides...	10	–	–	–
Veterinary assistants and laboratory animal caretakers..	7	–	–	–
Phlebotomists...	16	–	–	–
Miscellaneous healthcare support occupations, including medical equipment preparers.............	26	–	–	–
Protective service occupations............................	2,287	797	13	75.5
First-line supervisors of correctional officers........	30	–	–	–
First-line supervisors of police and detectives.......	83	1,109	147	–
First-line supervisors of fire fighting and prevention workers..	39	–	–	–
First-line supervisors of protective service workers, all other...	73	788	51	–
Firefighters..	281	998	29	–
Fire inspectors..	17	–	–	–
Bailiffs, correctional officers, and jailers..............	320	722	20	81.2
Detectives and criminal investigators.................	125	1,192	57	–
Fish and game wardens..................................	5	–	–	–
Parking enforcement workers............................	3	–	–	–
Police and sheriff's patrol officers......................	578	948	24	98.9
Transit and railroad police...............................	7	–	–	–
Animal control workers....................................	5	–	–	–
Private detectives and investigators....................	56	891	69	–

See note at end of table.

Occupation	Both sexes			Women		
	Number of workers (in thousands)	Median weekly earnings	Standard error of median	Number of workers (in thousands)	Median weekly earnings	Standard error of median
Security guards and gaming surveillance officers..	775	$519	$9	156	$474	$19
Crossing guards	23	–	–	8	–	–
Transportation security screeners	21	–	–	10	–	–
Lifeguards and other recreational, and all other protective service workers	44	–	–	23	–	–
Food preparation and serving related occupations	3,930	409	3	1,909	390	4
Chefs and head cooks	299	580	17	53	502	25
First-line supervisors of food preparation and serving workers	378	485	20	220	458	20
Cooks	1,210	390	5	449	363	7
Food preparation workers	357	384	11	202	375	13
Bartenders	210	545	22	106	505	26
Combined food preparation and serving workers, including fast food	161	387	12	114	385	15
Counter attendants, cafeteria, food concession, and coffee shop	58	323	9	32	–	–
Waiters and waitresses	872	407	7	559	389	8
Food servers, nonrestaurant	84	419	22	52	393	24
Dining room and cafeteria attendants and bartender helpers	119	383	15	42	–	–
Dishwashers	118	332	14	28	–	–
Hosts and hostesses, restaurant, lounge, and coffee shop	62	369	20	52	356	18
Food preparation and serving related workers, all other	4	–	–	–	–	–
Building and grounds cleaning and maintenance occupations	3,339	465	6	1,128	406	5
First-line supervisors of housekeeping and janitorial workers	179	646	49	67	488	99
First-line supervisors of landscaping, lawn service, and groundskeeping workers	94	797	69	10	–	–
Janitors and building cleaners	1,496	489	6	384	418	8
Maids and housekeeping cleaners	751	399	7	638	392	6
Pest control workers	58	575	32	1	–	–
Grounds maintenance workers	761	425	11	29	–	–
Personal care and service occupations	2,121	453	9	1,543	422	5
First-line supervisors of gaming workers	90	739	45	39	–	–
First-line supervisors of personal service workers.	67	613	29	46	–	–
Animal trainers	16	–	–	7	–	–
Nonfarm animal caretakers	82	419	33	60	417	40
Gaming services workers	82	636	26	39	–	–
Motion picture projectionists	3	–	–	–	–	–
Ushers, lobby attendants, and ticket takers	9	–	–	6	–	–
Miscellaneous entertainment attendants and related workers	66	424	36	31	–	–
Embalmers and funeral attendants	5	–	–	2	–	–
Morticians, undertakers, and funeral directors	16	–	–	3	–	–
Barbers	29	–	–	4	–	–
Hairdressers, hairstylists, and cosmetologists	282	453	29	259	440	28
Miscellaneous personal appearance workers	136	441	35	104	413	15
Baggage porters, bellhops, and concierges	63	545	34	8	–	–
Tour and travel guides	9	–	–	3	–	–
Childcare workers	367	382	12	342	383	11
Personal care aides	549	412	7	455	407	7

See note at end of table.

Table 2. Median usual weekly earnings of full-time wage and salary workers, by detailed occupation and sex, 2011 annual averages—cont'd

Occupation	Men			Women's earnings as a percent of men's
	Number of workers (in thousands)	Median weekly earnings	Standard error of median	
Security guards and gaming surveillance officers..	619	$544	$21	87.1
Crossing guards..	15	–	–	–
Transportation security screeners.....................	12	–	–	–
Lifeguards and other recreational, and all other protective service workers.....................	21	–	–	–
Food preparation and serving related occupations......	2,021	429	7	90.9
Chefs and head cooks....................................	245	601	19	83.5
First-line supervisors of food preparation and serving workers...................................	158	525	37	87.2
Cooks...	761	406	6	89.4
Food preparation workers...............................	155	395	16	94.9
Bartenders..	104	593	16	85.2
Combined food preparation and serving workers, including fast food.....................................	46	–	–	–
Counter attendants, cafeteria, food concession, and coffee shop.......................................	26	–	–	–
Waiters and waitresses..................................	313	466	29	83.5
Food servers, nonrestaurant............................	31	–	–	–
Dining room and cafeteria attendants and bartender helpers......................................	77	392	17	–
Dishwashers..	90	321	7	–
Hosts and hostesses, restaurant, lounge, and coffee shop..	10	–	–	–
Food preparation and serving related workers, all other..	4	–	–	–
Building and grounds cleaning and maintenance occupations...	2,212	502	6	80.9
First-line supervisors of housekeeping and janitorial workers.....................................	113	756	42	64.6
First-line supervisors of landscaping, lawn service, and groundskeeping workers..............	85	808	66	–
Janitors and building cleaners..........................	1,111	514	7	81.3
Maids and housekeeping cleaners.....................	114	473	25	82.9
Pest control workers......................................	57	572	35	–
Grounds maintenance workers..........................	732	424	10	–
Personal care and service occupations....................	578	562	26	75.1
First-line supervisors of gaming workers.............	51	876	59	–
First-line supervisors of personal service workers.	21	–	–	–
Animal trainers...	9	–	–	–
Nonfarm animal caretakers.............................	22	–	–	–
Gaming services workers................................	43	–	–	–
Motion picture projectionists...........................	3	–	–	–
Ushers, lobby attendants, and ticket takers.........	3	–	–	–
Miscellaneous entertainment attendants and related workers..	35	–	–	–
Embalmers and funeral attendants....................	3	–	–	–
Morticians, undertakers, and funeral directors......	12	–	–	–
Barbers..	25	–	–	–
Hairdressers, hairstylists, and cosmetologists......	23	–	–	–
Miscellaneous personal appearance workers.......	32	–	–	–
Baggage porters, bellhops, and concierges.........	55	561	32	–
Tour and travel guides...................................	6	–	–	–
Childcare workers...	26	–	–	–
Personal care aides......................................	94	454	37	89.6

See note at end of table.

Table 2. Median usual weekly earnings of full-time wage and salary workers, by detailed occupation and sex, 2011 annual averages—cont'd

Occupation	Both sexes			Women		
	Number of workers (in thousands)	Median weekly earnings	Standard error of median	Number of workers (in thousands)	Median weekly earnings	Standard error of median
Recreation and fitness workers	177	$506	$17	101	$494	$15
Residential advisors	42	–	–	27	–	–
Personal care and service workers, all other	34	–	–	11	–	–
Sales and office occupations	22,989	638	3	13,977	602	2
Sales and related occupations	9,294	670	6	4,069	549	9
First-line supervisors of retail sales workers	2,223	676	11	959	599	9
First-line supervisors of non-retail sales workers	702	951	21	214	781	56
Cashiers	1,343	383	5	962	373	5
Counter and rental clerks	87	603	33	38	–	–
Parts salespersons	117	610	29	16	–	–
Retail salespersons	1,789	545	14	733	466	13
Advertising sales agents	202	893	37	112	772	81
Insurance sales agents	384	807	27	201	665	21
Securities, commodities, and financial services sales agents	222	1,144	52	73	884	275
Travel agents	49	–	–	38	–	–
Sales representatives, services, all other	397	887	30	119	757	37
Sales representatives, wholesale and manufacturing	1,091	991	26	262	927	33
Models, demonstrators, and product promoters	15	–	–	11	–	–
Real estate brokers and sales agents	380	812	50	204	676	51
Sales engineers	30	–	–	3	–	–
Telemarketers	69	412	18	40	–	–
Door-to-door sales workers, news and street vendors, and related workers	55	526	80	20	–	–
Sales and related workers, all other	140	781	136	64	618	28
Office and administrative support occupations	13,695	623	3	9,908	615	3
First-line supervisors of office and administrative support workers	1,274	764	10	856	741	11
Switchboard operators, including answering service	29	–	–	25	–	–
Telephone operators	38	–	–	30	–	–
Communications equipment operators, all other	6	–	–	3	–	–
Bill and account collectors	178	608	12	130	597	12
Billing and posting clerks	397	607	10	359	605	10
Bookkeeping, accounting, and auditing clerks	862	655	12	750	656	13
Gaming cage workers	2	–	–	1	–	–
Payroll and timekeeping clerks	136	710	23	125	704	25
Procurement clerks	24	–	–	16	–	–
Tellers	283	492	9	241	500	8
Financial clerks, all other	64	793	142	48	–	–
Brokerage clerks	11	–	–	4	–	–
Correspondence clerks	10	–	–	8	–	–
Court, municipal, and license clerks	74	763	33	60	738	29
Credit authorizers, checkers, and clerks	47	–	–	34	–	–
Customer service representatives	1,509	588	8	972	569	9
Eligibility interviewers, government programs	79	632	52	70	632	49
File clerks	248	616	16	217	620	18
Hotel, motel, and resort desk clerks	86	423	25	53	416	22
Interviewers, except eligibility and loan	121	546	23	99	551	24
Library assistants, clerical	49	–	–	38	–	–
Loan interviewers and clerks	110	706	39	93	696	43
New accounts clerks	27	–	–	19	–	–
Order clerks	96	586	39	60	577	68

See note at end of table.

Table 2. **Median usual weekly earnings of full-time wage and salary workers, by detailed occupation and sex, 2011 annual averages—cont'd**

Occupation	Men			Women's earnings as a percent of men's
	Number of workers (in thousands)	Median weekly earnings	Standard error of median	
Recreation and fitness workers	76	$575	$51	85.9
Residential advisors	15	–	–	–
Personal care and service workers, all other	23	–	–	–
Sales and office occupations	9,012	738	6	81.6
Sales and related occupations	5,225	804	15	68.3
First-line supervisors of retail sales workers	1,263	759	11	78.9
First-line supervisors of non-retail sales workers	488	1,016	36	76.9
Cashiers	381	411	10	90.8
Counter and rental clerks	50	620	62	–
Parts salespersons	100	587	41	–
Retail salespersons	1,056	620	13	75.2
Advertising sales agents	90	961	25	80.3
Insurance sales agents	183	1,033	39	64.4
Securities, commodities, and financial services sales agents	149	1,269	199	69.7
Travel agents	11	–	–	–
Sales representatives, services, all other	278	953	32	79.4
Sales representatives, wholesale and manufacturing	829	1,019	31	91.0
Models, demonstrators, and product promoters	4	–	–	–
Real estate brokers and sales agents	176	992	31	68.1
Sales engineers	27	–	–	–
Telemarketers	29	–	–	–
Door-to-door sales workers, news and street vendors, and related workers	35	–	–	–
Sales and related workers, all other	76	985	42	62.7
Office and administrative support occupations	3,787	668	10	92.1
First-line supervisors of office and administrative support workers	418	833	29	89.0
Switchboard operators, including answering service	4	–	–	–
Telephone operators	7	–	–	–
Communications equipment operators, all other	4	–	–	–
Bill and account collectors	48	–	–	–
Billing and posting clerks	38	–	–	–
Bookkeeping, accounting, and auditing clerks	112	654	25	100.3
Gaming cage workers	1	–	–	–
Payroll and timekeeping clerks	11	–	–	–
Procurement clerks	9	–	–	–
Tellers	41	–	–	–
Financial clerks, all other	16	–	–	–
Brokerage clerks	7	–	–	–
Correspondence clerks	2	–	–	–
Court, municipal, and license clerks	14	–	–	–
Credit authorizers, checkers, and clerks	13	–	–	–
Customer service representatives	538	628	22	90.6
Eligibility interviewers, government programs	9	–	–	–
File clerks	32	–	–	–
Hotel, motel, and resort desk clerks	33	–	–	–
Interviewers, except eligibility and loan	21	–	–	–
Library assistants, clerical	12	–	–	–
Loan interviewers and clerks	17	–	–	–
New accounts clerks	8	–	–	–
Order clerks	35	–	–	–

See note at end of table.

Table 2. Median usual weekly earnings of full-time wage and salary workers, by detailed occupation and sex, 2011 annual averages—cont'd

Occupation	Both sexes			Women		
	Number of workers (in thousands)	Median weekly earnings	Standard error of median	Number of workers (in thousands)	Median weekly earnings	Standard error of median
Human resources assistants, except payroll and timekeeping	45	–	–	40	–	–
Receptionists and information clerks	868	$520	$6	790	$520	$6
Reservation and transportation ticket agents and travel clerks	80	649	169	47	–	–
Information and record clerks, all other	105	744	25	86	737	23
Cargo and freight agents	6	–	–	2	–	–
Couriers and messengers	164	744	41	19	–	–
Dispatchers	207	651	20	126	626	20
Meter readers, utilities	21	–	–	3	–	–
Postal service clerks	129	978	16	63	892	33
Postal service mail carriers	303	979	26	98	892	35
Postal service mail sorters, processors, and processing machine operators	57	918	39	24	–	–
Production, planning, and expediting clerks	226	812	23	116	722	41
Shipping, receiving, and traffic clerks	481	562	17	141	543	27
Stock clerks and order fillers	992	492	7	337	501	12
Weighers, measurers, checkers, and samplers, recordkeeping	60	596	75	28	–	–
Secretaries and administrative assistants	2,143	654	7	2,059	651	7
Computer operators	116	724	48	56	651	83
Data entry keyers	280	595	12	231	597	12
Word processors and typists	109	599	22	99	594	20
Desktop publishers	1	–	–	–	–	–
Insurance claims and policy processing clerks	236	660	19	197	647	20
Mail clerks and mail machine operators, except postal service	79	521	24	41	–	–
Office clerks, general	794	604	9	673	594	9
Office machine operators, except computer	31	–	–	20	–	–
Proofreaders and copy markers	7	–	–	6	–	–
Statistical assistants	12	–	–	8	–	–
Office and administrative support workers, all other	387	679	17	286	645	26
Natural resources, construction, and maintenance occupations	9,965	732	6	391	515	16
Farming, fishing, and forestry occupations	775	430	10	150	371	10
First-line supervisors of farming, fishing, and forestry workers	38	–	–	3	–	–
Agricultural inspectors	23	–	–	12	–	–
Animal breeders	3	–	–	1	–	–
Graders and sorters, agricultural products	85	379	28	53	363	12
Miscellaneous agricultural workers	565	419	7	77	370	15
Fishers and related fishing workers	13	–	–	–	–	–
Hunters and trappers	1	–	–	–	–	–
Forest and conservation workers	8	–	–	4	–	–
Logging workers	39	–	–	–	–	–
Construction and extraction occupations	5,031	717	7	95	612	60
First-line supervisors of construction trades and extraction workers	482	992	21	15	–	–
Boilermakers	18	–	–	–	–	–
Brickmasons, blockmasons, and stonemasons	96	710	44	1	–	–
Carpenters	737	630	16	10	–	–
Carpet, floor, and tile installers and finishers	110	579	31	1	–	–

See note at end of table.

Table 2. **Median usual weekly earnings of full-time wage and salary workers, by detailed occupation and sex, 2011 annual averages—cont'd**

Occupation	Men			Women's earnings as a percent of men's
	Number of workers (in thousands)	Median weekly earnings	Standard error of median	
Human resources assistants, except payroll and timekeeping	5	–	–	–
Receptionists and information clerks	78	$521	$21	99.8
Reservation and transportation ticket agents and travel clerks	33	–	–	–
Information and record clerks, all other	18	–	–	–
Cargo and freight agents	4	–	–	–
Couriers and messengers	145	785	104	–
Dispatchers	81	728	43	86.0
Meter readers, utilities	18	–	–	–
Postal service clerks	66	1,014	21	88.0
Postal service mail carriers	205	1,017	28	87.7
Postal service mail sorters, processors, and processing machine operators	33	–	–	–
Production, planning, and expediting clerks	110	916	33	78.8
Shipping, receiving, and traffic clerks	340	571	19	95.1
Stock clerks and order fillers	655	488	9	102.7
Weighers, measurers, checkers, and samplers, recordkeeping	32	–	–	–
Secretaries and administrative assistants	84	757	36	86.0
Computer operators	59	853	86	76.3
Data entry keyers	49	–	–	–
Word processors and typists	10	–	–	–
Desktop publishers	1	–	–	–
Insurance claims and policy processing clerks	39	–	–	–
Mail clerks and mail machine operators, except postal service	38	–	–	–
Office clerks, general	121	712	30	83.4
Office machine operators, except computer	11	–	–	–
Proofreaders and copy markers	1	–	–	–
Statistical assistants	4	–	–	–
Office and administrative support workers, all other	101	792	57	81.4
Natural resources, construction, and maintenance occupations	9,574	740	6	69.6
Farming, fishing, and forestry occupations	625	445	10	83.4
First-line supervisors of farming, fishing, and forestry workers	35	–	–	–
Agricultural inspectors	11	–	–	–
Animal breeders	2	–	–	–
Graders and sorters, agricultural products	32	–	–	–
Miscellaneous agricultural workers	488	427	10	86.7
Fishers and related fishing workers	13	–	–	–
Hunters and trappers	1	–	–	–
Forest and conservation workers	4	–	–	–
Logging workers	39	–	–	–
Construction and extraction occupations	4,937	718	8	85.2
First-line supervisors of construction trades and extraction workers	467	1,001	21	–
Boilermakers	18	–	–	–
Brickmasons, blockmasons, and stonemasons	95	706	43	–
Carpenters	727	630	16	–
Carpet, floor, and tile installers and finishers	109	581	28	–

See note at end of table.

Table 2. Median usual weekly earnings of full-time wage and salary workers, by detailed occupation and sex, 2011 annual averages—cont'd

Occupation	Both sexes			Women		
	Number of workers (in thousands)	Median weekly earnings	Standard error of median	Number of workers (in thousands)	Median weekly earnings	Standard error of median
Cement masons, concrete finishers, and terrazzo workers...	59	$651	$31	–	–	–
Construction laborers.......................................	862	586	10	15	–	–
Paving, surfacing, and tamping equipment operators...	19	–	–	–	–	–
Pile-driver operators.......................................	1	–	–	–	–	–
Operating engineers and other construction equipment operators.................................	345	809	29	2	–	–
Drywall installers, ceiling tile installers, and tapers.	101	507	19	1	–	–
Electricians...	542	857	30	3	–	–
Glaziers..	40	–	–	–	–	–
Insulation workers..	41	–	–	2	–	–
Painters, construction and maintenance..............	266	544	29	17	–	–
Paperhangers..	2	–	–	–	–	–
Pipelayers, plumbers, pipefitters, and steamfitters.	417	851	26	11	–	–
Plasterers and stucco masons..........................	13	–	–	–	–	–
Reinforcing iron and rebar workers....................	5	–	–	–	–	–
Roofers..	143	523	27	3	–	–
Sheet metal workers...	107	805	40	3	–	–
Structural iron and steel workers.......................	66	870	44	–	–	–
Solar photovoltaic installers..............................	2	–	–	–	–	–
Helpers, construction trades..............................	50	469	37	3	–	–
Construction and building inspectors..................	54	906	49	2	–	–
Elevator installers and repairers........................	30	–	–	–	–	–
Fence erectors...	32	–	–	–	–	–
Hazardous materials removal workers................	25	–	–	1	–	–
Highway maintenance workers...........................	96	708	31	2	–	–
Rail-track laying and maintenance equipment operators...	8	–	–	–	–	–
Septic tank servicers and sewer pipe cleaners......	9	–	–	–	–	–
Miscellaneous construction and related workers...	28	–	–	–	–	–
Derrick, rotary drill, and service unit operators, oil, gas, and mining...................................	42	–	–	–	–	–
Earth drillers, except oil and gas.......................	17	–	–	–	–	–
Explosives workers, ordnance handling experts, and blasters...	10	–	–	–	–	–
Mining machine operators.................................	70	1,022	71	1	–	–
Roof bolters, mining...	12	–	–	–	–	–
Roustabouts, oil and gas..................................	18	–	–	1	–	–
Helpers—extraction workers.............................	8	–	–	–	–	–
Other extraction workers...................................	49	–	–	–	–	–
Installation, maintenance, and repair occupations.......	4,159	806	7	146	$751	$33
First-line supervisors of mechanics, installers, and repairers...	327	947	34	21	–	–
Computer, automated teller, and office machine repairers...	237	811	23	22	–	–
Radio and telecommunications equipment installers and repairers...........................	139	898	35	12	–	–
Avionics technicians...	16	–	–	2	–	–
Electric motor, power tool, and related repairers...	26	–	–	–	–	–
Electrical and electronics installers and repairers, transportation equipment..................	7	–	–	–	–	–
Electrical and electronics repairers, industrial and utility...	15	–	–	1	–	–

See note at end of table.

Table 2. **Median usual weekly earnings of full-time wage and salary workers, by detailed occupation and sex, 2011 annual averages—cont'd**

Occupation	Men			Women's earnings as a percent of men's
	Number of workers (in thousands)	Median weekly earnings	Standard error of median	
Cement masons, concrete finishers, and terrazzo workers	59	$651	$31	–
Construction laborers	846	587	10	–
Paving, surfacing, and tamping equipment operators	18	–	–	–
Pile-driver operators	1	–	–	–
Operating engineers and other construction equipment operators	343	809	29	–
Drywall installers, ceiling tile installers, and tapers	100	509	19	–
Electricians	539	855	30	–
Glaziers	40	–	–	–
Insulation workers	39	–	–	–
Painters, construction and maintenance	249	555	30	–
Paperhangers	2	–	–	–
Pipelayers, plumbers, pipefitters, and steamfitters	406	853	26	–
Plasterers and stucco masons	13	–	–	–
Reinforcing iron and rebar workers	5	–	–	–
Roofers	141	520	24	–
Sheet metal workers	104	805	39	–
Structural iron and steel workers	66	870	44	–
Solar photovoltaic installers	2	–	–	–
Helpers, construction trades	47	–	–	–
Construction and building inspectors	52	919	55	–
Elevator installers and repairers	30	–	–	–
Fence erectors	32	–	–	–
Hazardous materials removal workers	24	–	–	–
Highway maintenance workers	94	711	41	–
Rail-track laying and maintenance equipment operators	8	–	–	–
Septic tank servicers and sewer pipe cleaners	9	–	–	–
Miscellaneous construction and related workers	28	–	–	–
Derrick, rotary drill, and service unit operators, oil, gas, and mining	42	–	–	–
Earth drillers, except oil and gas	17	–	–	–
Explosives workers, ordnance handling experts, and blasters	10	–	–	–
Mining machine operators	69	1,010	83	–
Roof bolters, mining	12	–	–	–
Roustabouts, oil and gas	17	–	–	–
Helpers—extraction workers	8	–	–	–
Other extraction workers	49	–	–	–
Installation, maintenance, and repair occupations	4,013	807	7	93.1
First-line supervisors of mechanics, installers, and repairers	306	936	38	–
Computer, automated teller, and office machine repairers	215	812	22	–
Radio and telecommunications equipment installers and repairers	127	883	33	–
Avionics technicians	15	–	–	–
Electric motor, power tool, and related repairers	25	–	–	–
Electrical and electronics installers and repairers, transportation equipment	7	–	–	–
Electrical and electronics repairers, industrial and utility	14	–	–	–

See note at end of table.

Table 2. Median usual weekly earnings of full-time wage and salary workers, by detailed occupation and sex, 2011 annual averages—cont'd

Occupation	Both sexes			Women		
	Number of workers (in thousands)	Median weekly earnings	Standard error of median	Number of workers (in thousands)	Median weekly earnings	Standard error of median
Electronic equipment installers and repairers, motor vehicles..	14	–	–	–	–	–
Electronic home entertainment equipment installers and repairers..................................	32	–	–	2	–	–
Security and fire alarm systems installers............	44	–	–	–	–	–
Aircraft mechanics and service technicians..........	143	$988	$38	4	–	–
Automotive body and related repairers................	107	624	28	1	–	–
Automotive glass installers and repairers............	11	–	–	–	–	–
Automotive service technicians and mechanics.....	653	714	18	8	–	–
Bus and truck mechanics and diesel engine specialists..	286	801	21	1	–	–
Heavy vehicle and mobile equipment service technicians and mechanics............................	182	822	38	3	–	–
Small engine mechanics.................................	32	–	–	1	–	–
Miscellaneous vehicle and mobile equipment mechanics, installers, and repairers................	73	463	33	2	–	–
Control and valve installers and repairers............	25	–	–	1	–	–
Heating, air conditioning, and refrigeration mechanics and installers...............................	281	793	27	1	–	–
Home appliance repairers...............................	27	–	–	4	–	–
Industrial and refractory machinery mechanics.....	425	868	30	10	–	–
Maintenance and repair workers, general............	359	758	18	11	–	–
Maintenance workers, machinery.......................	34	–	–	3	–	–
Millwrights...	57	892	29	1	–	–
Electrical power-line installers and repairers.........	111	1,116	47	–	–	–
Telecommunications line installers and repairers...	192	915	55	7	–	–
Precision instrument and equipment repairers......	62	898	48	10	–	–
Wind turbine service technicians......................	2	–	–	–	–	–
Coin, vending, and amusement machine servicers and repairers...............................	29	–	–	1	–	–
Commercial divers..	1	–	–	–	–	–
Locksmiths and safe repairers.........................	17	–	–	1	–	–
Manufactured building and mobile home installers.	7	–	–	–	–	–
Riggers..	15	–	–	3	–	–
Signal and track switch repairers......................	5	–	–	–	–	–
Helpers—installation, maintenance, and repair workers..	18	–	–	1	–	–
Other installation, maintenance, and repair workers..	149	671	46	12	–	–
Production, transportation, and material moving occupations...	13,333	609	3	2,603	$485	$5
Production occupations..................................	7,058	605	4	1,817	483	6
First-line supervisors of production and operating workers......................................	654	888	25	124	665	38
Aircraft structure, surfaces, rigging, and systems assemblers..	19	–	–	7	–	–
Electrical, electronics, and electromechanical assemblers..	148	521	27	73	449	20
Engine and other machine assemblers...............	30	–	–	4	–	–
Structural metal fabricators and fitters................	33	–	–	1	–	–
Miscellaneous assemblers and fabricators..........	758	519	9	285	479	14
Bakers...	125	448	17	63	416	28
Butchers and other meat, poultry, and fish processing workers....................................	281	504	9	66	479	13

See note at end of table.

Table 2. **Median usual weekly earnings of full-time wage and salary workers, by detailed occupation and sex, 2011 annual averages—cont'd**

Occupation	Men			Women's earnings as a percent of men's
	Number of workers (in thousands)	Median weekly earnings	Standard error of median	
Electronic equipment installers and repairers, motor vehicles..	14	–	–	–
Electronic home entertainment equipment installers and repairers.............................	30	–	–	–
Security and fire alarm systems installers...........	44	–	–	–
Aircraft mechanics and service technicians.........	139	$990	$38	–
Automotive body and related repairers...............	107	625	29	–
Automotive glass installers and repairers...........	10	–	–	–
Automotive service technicians and mechanics....	645	718	19	–
Bus and truck mechanics and diesel engine specialists..	286	802	21	–
Heavy vehicle and mobile equipment service technicians and mechanics............................	179	822	38	–
Small engine mechanics...................................	31	–	–	–
Miscellaneous vehicle and mobile equipment mechanics, installers, and repairers..................	71	463	33	–
Control and valve installers and repairers...........	24	–	–	–
Heating, air conditioning, and refrigeration mechanics and installers..............................	279	795	27	–
Home appliance repairers.................................	23	–	–	–
Industrial and refractory machinery mechanics.....	415	870	31	–
Maintenance and repair workers, general...........	347	756	18	–
Maintenance workers, machinery.......................	31	–	–	–
Millwrights..	56	897	28	–
Electrical power-line installers and repairers........	111	1,116	47	–
Telecommunications line installers and repairers...	185	926	56	–
Precision instrument and equipment repairers......	52	914	44	–
Wind turbine service technicians.......................	2	–	–	–
Coin, vending, and amusement machine servicers and repairers.................................	27	–	–	–
Commercial divers...	1	–	–	–
Locksmiths and safe repairers..........................	17	–	–	–
Manufactured building and mobile home installers.	7	–	–	–
Riggers..	12	–	–	–
Signal and track switch repairers......................	5	–	–	–
Helpers—installation, maintenance, and repair workers..	17	–	–	–
Other installation, maintenance, and repair workers..	137	718	55	–
Production, transportation, and material moving occupations..	10,730	651	5	74.5
Production occupations....................................	5,241	667	7	72.4
First-line supervisors of production and operating workers......................................	530	929	24	71.6
Aircraft structure, surfaces, rigging, and systems assemblers...................................	13	–	–	–
Electrical, electronics, and electromechanical assemblers..	75	591	24	76.0
Engine and other machine assemblers...............	25	–	–	–
Structural metal fabricators and fitters...............	31	–	–	–
Miscellaneous assemblers and fabricators..........	473	566	22	84.6
Bakers...	63	471	20	88.3
Butchers and other meat, poultry, and fish processing workers.....................................	215	515	11	93.0

See note at end of table.

29

Table 2. Median usual weekly earnings of full-time wage and salary workers, by detailed occupation and sex, 2011 annual averages—cont'd

Occupation	Both sexes			Women		
	Number of workers (in thousands)	Median weekly earnings	Standard error of median	Number of workers (in thousands)	Median weekly earnings	Standard error of median
Food and tobacco roasting, baking, and drying machine operators and tenders	7	–	–	3	–	–
Food batchmakers	63	$554	$28	28	–	–
Food cooking machine operators and tenders	17	–	–	5	–	–
Food processing workers, all other	104	534	20	25	–	–
Computer control programmers and operators	70	770	52	5	–	–
Extruding and drawing machine setters, operators, and tenders, metal and plastic	11	–	–	2	–	–
Forging machine setters, operators, and tenders, metal and plastic	5	–	–	1	–	–
Rolling machine setters, operators, and tenders, metal and plastic	9	–	–	2	–	–
Cutting, punching, and press machine setters, operators, and tenders, metal and plastic	92	591	23	15	–	–
Drilling and boring machine tool setters, operators, and tenders, metal and plastic	5	–	–	1	–	–
Grinding, lapping, polishing, and buffing machine tool setters, operators, and tenders, metal and plastic	60	643	60	3	–	–
Lathe and turning machine tool setters, operators, and tenders, metal and plastic	15	–	–	–	–	–
Milling and planing machine setters, operators, and tenders, metal and plastic	3	–	–	–	–	–
Machinists	393	755	20	16	–	–
Metal furnace operators, tenders, pourers, and casters	19	–	–	1	–	–
Model makers and patternmakers, metal and plastic	4	–	–	1	–	–
Molders and molding machine setters, operators, and tenders, metal and plastic	47	–	–	12	–	–
Multiple machine tool setters, operators, and tenders, metal and plastic	3	–	–	–	–	–
Tool and die makers	61	920	48	2	–	–
Welding, soldering, and brazing workers	461	679	21	36	–	–
Heat treating equipment setters, operators, and tenders, metal and plastic	5	–	–	1	–	–
Layout workers, metal and plastic	8	–	–	1	–	–
Plating and coating machine setters, operators, and tenders, metal and plastic	15	–	–	2	–	–
Tool grinders, filers, and sharpeners	6	–	–	–	–	–
Metal workers and plastic workers, all other	356	561	19	81	$517	$31
Prepress technicians and workers	30	–	–	16	–	–
Printing press operators	186	613	23	31	–	–
Print binding and finishing workers	13	–	–	6	–	–
Laundry and dry-cleaning workers	115	412	20	64	386	25
Pressers, textile, garment, and related materials	37	–	–	24	–	–
Sewing machine operators	112	403	17	84	398	18
Shoe and leather workers and repairers	8	–	–	1	–	–
Shoe machine operators and tenders	2	–	–	1	–	–
Tailors, dressmakers, and sewers	46	–	–	33	–	–
Textile bleaching and dyeing machine operators and tenders	4	–	–	–	–	–
Textile cutting machine setters, operators, and tenders	6	–	–	2	–	–

See note at end of table.

Table 2. **Median usual weekly earnings of full-time wage and salary workers, by detailed occupation and sex, 2011 annual averages—cont'd**

Occupation	Men			Women's earnings as a percent of men's
	Number of workers (in thousands)	Median weekly earnings	Standard error of median	
Food and tobacco roasting, baking, and drying machine operators and tenders	5	–	–	–
Food batchmakers	35	–	–	–
Food cooking machine operators and tenders	12	–	–	–
Food processing workers, all other	78	$544	$22	–
Computer control programmers and operators	65	781	55	–
Extruding and drawing machine setters, operators, and tenders, metal and plastic	9	–	–	–
Forging machine setters, operators, and tenders, metal and plastic	4	–	–	–
Rolling machine setters, operators, and tenders, metal and plastic	7	–	–	–
Cutting, punching, and press machine setters, operators, and tenders, metal and plastic	78	608	24	–
Drilling and boring machine tool setters, operators, and tenders, metal and plastic	4	–	–	–
Grinding, lapping, polishing, and buffing machine tool setters, operators, and tenders, metal and plastic	57	641	58	–
Lathe and turning machine tool setters, operators, and tenders, metal and plastic	15	–	–	–
Milling and planing machine setters, operators, and tenders, metal and plastic	3	–	–	–
Machinists	377	767	20	–
Metal furnace operators, tenders, pourers, and casters	18	–	–	–
Model makers and patternmakers, metal and plastic	3	–	–	–
Molders and molding machine setters, operators, and tenders, metal and plastic	35	–	–	–
Multiple machine tool setters, operators, and tenders, metal and plastic	3	–	–	–
Tool and die makers	59	930	48	–
Welding, soldering, and brazing workers	426	695	21	–
Heat treating equipment setters, operators, and tenders, metal and plastic	4	–	–	–
Layout workers, metal and plastic	7	–	–	–
Plating and coating machine setters, operators, and tenders, metal and plastic	13	–	–	–
Tool grinders, filers, and sharpeners	6	–	–	–
Metal workers and plastic workers, all other	275	583	16	88.7
Prepress technicians and workers	14	–	–	–
Printing press operators	155	646	31	–
Print binding and finishing workers	7	–	–	–
Laundry and dry-cleaning workers	52	447	32	86.4
Pressers, textile, garment, and related materials	13	–	–	–
Sewing machine operators	28	–	–	–
Shoe and leather workers and repairers	7	–	–	–
Shoe machine operators and tenders	1	–	–	–
Tailors, dressmakers, and sewers	13	–	–	–
Textile bleaching and dyeing machine operators and tenders	4	–	–	–
Textile cutting machine setters, operators, and tenders	4	–	–	–

See note at end of table.

Occupation	Both sexes			Women		
	Number of workers (in thousands)	Median weekly earnings	Standard error of median	Number of workers (in thousands)	Median weekly earnings	Standard error of median
Textile knitting and weaving machine setters, operators, and tenders...........................	8	–	–	6	–	–
Textile winding, twisting, and drawing out machine setters, operators, and tenders...........	19	–	–	11	–	–
Extruding and forming machine setters, operators, and tenders, synthetic and glass fibers..............	2	–	–	–	–	–
Fabric and apparel patternmakers....................	5	–	–	2	–	–
Upholsterers..	34	–	–	4	–	–
Textile, apparel, and furnishings workers, all other.	15	–	–	5	–	–
Cabinetmakers and bench carpenters................	42	–	–	1	–	–
Furniture finishers..	11	–	–	2	–	–
Model makers and patternmakers, wood.............	1	–	–	–	–	–
Sawing machine setters, operators, and tenders, wood..	31	–	–	1	–	–
Woodworking machine setters, operators, and tenders, except sawing.............................	17	–	–	2	–	–
Woodworkers, all other..................................	10	–	–	2	–	–
Power plant operators, distributors, and dispatchers..	53	$1,091	$101	1	–	–
Stationary engineers and boiler operators...........	93	855	39	1	–	–
Water and wastewater treatment plant and system operators.......................................	75	780	57	5	–	–
Miscellaneous plant and system operators..........	37	–	–	3	–	–
Chemical processing machine setters, operators, and tenders................................	66	853	68	14	–	–
Crushing, grinding, polishing, mixing, and blending workers.......................................	94	659	46	12	–	–
Cutting workers..	69	518	27	13	–	–
Extruding, forming, pressing, and compacting machine setters, operators, and tenders...........	31	–	–	3	–	–
Furnace, kiln, oven, drier, and kettle operators and tenders..	11	–	–	–	–	–
Inspectors, testers, sorters, samplers, and weighers...	608	675	20	212	$541	$18
Jewelers and precious stone and metal workers...	14	–	–	7	–	–
Medical, dental, and ophthalmic laboratory technicians...	68	612	26	34	–	–
Packaging and filling machine operators and tenders...	259	455	22	139	421	12
Painting workers...	111	602	33	12	–	–
Photographic process workers and processing machine operators....................................	24	–	–	13	–	–
Semiconductor processors..............................	4	–	–	1	–	–
Adhesive bonding machine operators and tenders.	10	–	–	6	–	–
Cleaning, washing, and metal pickling equipment operators and tenders..................	13	–	–	3	–	–
Cooling and freezing equipment operators and tenders...	3	–	–	–	–	–
Etchers and engravers...................................	7	–	–	2	–	–
Molders, shapers, and casters, except metal and plastic...	21	–	–	6	–	–
Paper goods machine setters, operators, and tenders...	31	–	–	8	–	–
Tire builders...	17	–	–	1	–	–

See note at end of table.

Table 2. **Median usual weekly earnings of full-time wage and salary workers, by detailed occupation and sex, 2011 annual averages—cont'd**

Occupation	Men			Women's earnings as a percent of men's
	Number of workers (in thousands)	Median weekly earnings	Standard error of median	
Textile knitting and weaving machine setters, operators, and tenders..............................	2	–	–	–
Textile winding, twisting, and drawing out machine setters, operators, and tenders...........	8	–	–	–
Extruding and forming machine setters, operators, and tenders, synthetic and glass fibers............	2	–	–	–
Fabric and apparel patternmakers....................	2	–	–	–
Upholsterers..	30	–	–	–
Textile, apparel, and furnishings workers, all other.	9	–	–	–
Cabinetmakers and bench carpenters................	41	–	–	–
Furniture finishers..	9	–	–	–
Model makers and patternmakers, wood.............	1	–	–	–
Sawing machine setters, operators, and tenders, wood...	30	–	–	–
Woodworking machine setters, operators, and tenders, except sawing..............................	15	–	–	–
Woodworkers, all other.....................................	8	–	–	–
Power plant operators, distributors, and dispatchers...	52	$1,085	$175	–
Stationary engineers and boiler operators...........	92	851	39	–
Water and wastewater treatment plant and system operators..	70	788	64	–
Miscellaneous plant and system operators..........	34	–	–	–
Chemical processing machine setters, operators, and tenders...................................	52	947	95	–
Crushing, grinding, polishing, mixing, and blending workers...	82	702	42	–
Cutting workers..	55	540	38	–
Extruding, forming, pressing, and compacting machine setters, operators, and tenders...........	28	–	–	–
Furnace, kiln, oven, drier, and kettle operators and tenders...	11	–	–	–
Inspectors, testers, sorters, samplers, and weighers..	396	792	39	68.3
Jewelers and precious stone and metal workers...	7	–	–	–
Medical, dental, and ophthalmic laboratory technicians...	34	–	–	–
Packaging and filling machine operators and tenders..	120	505	25	83.4
Painting workers...	99	608	36	–
Photographic process workers and processing machine operators...	10	–	–	–
Semiconductor processors................................	3	–	–	–
Adhesive bonding machine operators and tenders.	4	–	–	–
Cleaning, washing, and metal pickling equipment operators and tenders....................	9	–	–	–
Cooling and freezing equipment operators and tenders..	3	–	–	–
Etchers and engravers......................................	4	–	–	–
Molders, shapers, and casters, except metal and plastic..	15	–	–	–
Paper goods machine setters, operators, and tenders..	23	–	–	–
Tire builders..	16	–	–	–

See note at end of table.

Table 2. **Median usual weekly earnings of full-time wage and salary workers, by detailed occupation and sex, 2011 annual averages—cont'd**

Occupation	Both sexes			Women		
	Number of workers (in thousands)	Median weekly earnings	Standard error of median	Number of workers (in thousands)	Median weekly earnings	Standard error of median
Helpers—production workers............................	45	–	–	6	–	–
Production workers, all other...........................	652	$579	$11	151	$483	$15
Transportation and material moving occupations........	6,275	614	5	786	490	11
Supervisors of transportation and material moving workers..	208	761	25	38	–	–
Aircraft pilots and flight engineers.....................	93	1,461	221	4	–	–
Air traffic controllers and airfield operations specialists..	40	–	–	5	–	–
Flight attendants...	52	791	45	38	–	–
Ambulance drivers and attendants, except emergency medical technicians......................	9	–	–	–	–	–
Bus drivers...	310	608	14	122	579	17
Driver/sales workers and truck drivers...............	2,439	705	8	102	511	32
Taxi drivers and chauffeurs.............................	207	553	31	29	–	–
Motor vehicle operators, all other.....................	28	–	–	1	–	–
Locomotive engineers and operators.................	43	–	–	2	–	–
Railroad brake, signal, and switch operators........	6	–	–	–	–	–
Railroad conductors and yardmasters................	48	–	–	3	–	–
Subway, streetcar, and other rail transportation workers..	14	–	–	2	–	–
Sailors and marine oilers.................................	23	–	–	–	–	–
Ship and boat captains and operators................	35	–	–	–	–	–
Ship engineers...	6	–	–	–	–	–
Bridge and lock tenders..................................	7	–	–	–	–	–
Parking lot attendants....................................	46	–	–	5	–	–
Automotive and watercraft service attendants.......	42	–	–	2	–	–
Transportation inspectors................................	32	–	–	5	–	–
Transportation attendants, except flight attendants	13	–	–	8	–	–
Other transportation workers...........................	15	–	–	1	–	–
Conveyor operators and tenders......................	5	–	–	3	–	–
Crane and tower operators..............................	63	739	25	1	–	–
Dredge, excavating, and loading machine operators..	37	–	–	–	–	–
Hoist and winch operators...............................	5	–	–	2	–	–
Industrial truck and tractor operators..................	491	562	11	35	–	–
Cleaners of vehicles and equipment..................	230	465	23	25	–	–
Laborers and freight, stock, and material movers, hand..	1,260	509	7	175	416	13
Machine feeders and offbearers.......................	32	–	–	5	–	–
Packers and packagers, hand..........................	300	397	10	165	397	15
Pumping station operators...............................	26	–	–	–	–	–
Refuse and recyclable material collectors............	58	541	153	3	–	–
Mine shuttle car operators..............................	1	–	–	1	–	–
Tank car, truck, and ship loaders......................	3	–	–	–	–	–
Material moving workers, all other.....................	45	–	–	3	–	–

See note at end of table.

Table 2. **Median usual weekly earnings of full-time wage and salary workers, by detailed occupation and sex, 2011 annual averages—cont'd**

Occupation	Men			Women's earnings as a percent of men's
	Number of workers (in thousands)	Median weekly earnings	Standard error of median	
Helpers—production workers............................	40	–	–	–
Production workers, all other............................	502	$612	$13	78.9
Transportation and material moving occupations........	5,489	634	7	77.3
Supervisors of transportation and material moving workers..	170	773	64	–
Aircraft pilots and flight engineers......................	89	1,466	235	–
Air traffic controllers and airfield operations specialists..	35	–	–	–
Flight attendants...	14	–	–	–
Ambulance drivers and attendants, except emergency medical technicians.......................	9	–	–	–
Bus drivers...	188	645	31	89.8
Driver/sales workers and truck drivers................	2,337	712	8	71.8
Taxi drivers and chauffeurs...............................	178	576	33	–
Motor vehicle operators, all other......................	26	–	–	–
Locomotive engineers and operators..................	42	–	–	–
Railroad brake, signal, and switch operators........	6	–	–	–
Railroad conductors and yardmasters................	45	–	–	–
Subway, streetcar, and other rail transportation workers..	12	–	–	–
Sailors and marine oilers...................................	23	–	–	–
Ship and boat captains and operators................	35	–	–	–
Ship engineers...	6	–	–	–
Bridge and lock tenders....................................	7	–	–	–
Parking lot attendants.......................................	40	–	–	–
Automotive and watercraft service attendants.......	40	–	–	–
Transportation inspectors..................................	28	–	–	–
Transportation attendants, except flight attendants	5	–	–	–
Other transportation workers.............................	14	–	–	–
Conveyor operators and tenders........................	2	–	–	–
Crane and tower operators................................	62	736	25	–
Dredge, excavating, and loading machine operators...	37	–	–	–
Hoist and winch operators.................................	3	–	–	–
Industrial truck and tractor operators..................	456	556	11	–
Cleaners of vehicles and equipment...................	206	458	25	–
Laborers and freight, stock, and material movers, hand..	1,085	520	7	80.0
Machine feeders and offbearers.........................	27	–	–	–
Packers and packagers, hand............................	135	396	13	100.3
Pumping station operators.................................	26	–	–	–
Refuse and recyclable material collectors............	56	580	41	–
Mine shuttle car operators.................................	–	–	–	–
Tank car, truck, and ship loaders.......................	2	–	–	–
Material moving workers, all other......................	42	–	–	–

NOTE: Median earnings not shown where employment is less than 50,000. Women's earnings as a percent of men's not shown where employment for either the numerator or the denominator is less than 50,000.

Dash indicates no data or data that do not meet publication criteria.

SOURCE: U.S. Bureau of Labor Statistics.

Table 3. Median usual weekly earnings of full-time wage and salary workers, by state and sex, 2011 annual averages

State	Both sexes			Women		
	Number of workers (in thousands)	Median weekly earnings	Standard error of median	Number of workers (in thousands)	Median weekly earnings	Standard error of median
United States..................................	100,457	$756	$2	44,486	$684	$3
Alabama............................	1,476	680	14	675	595	13
Alaska................................	254	822	18	110	730	16
Arizona...............................	1,984	741	12	866	694	25
Arkansas............................	923	617	10	419	567	19
California............................	10,981	794	9	4,614	751	9
Colorado............................	1,724	845	17	716	740	16
Connecticut........................	1,197	988	24	526	878	33
Delaware............................	309	768	18	144	719	22
District of Columbia.....................	253	1,046	37	127	950	25
Florida...............................	6,041	736	6	2,869	668	9
Georgia..............................	3,250	723	13	1,504	641	14
Hawaii................................	422	738	15	201	657	16
Idaho.................................	450	700	13	178	604	10
Illinois................................	4,293	784	11	1,878	691	18
Indiana...............................	2,125	708	13	881	607	12
Iowa..................................	1,080	721	13	489	656	16
Kansas...............................	1,020	722	13	453	640	19
Kentucky............................	1,368	688	15	633	613	14
Louisiana...........................	1,423	709	23	633	592	13
Maine.................................	418	714	14	191	636	19
Maryland............................	2,146	885	24	1,014	815	25
Massachusetts....................	2,190	956	16	959	853	18
Michigan............................	2,857	781	11	1,252	685	18
Minnesota..........................	1,835	833	18	794	743	18
Mississippi.........................	887	644	13	418	582	17
Missouri.............................	2,036	733	13	955	628	15
Montana.............................	288	623	12	135	564	13
Nebraska...........................	659	701	14	301	631	21
Nevada..............................	841	697	13	364	650	16
New Hampshire....................	482	862	18	213	748	19
New Jersey.........................	3,090	926	15	1,373	831	20
New Mexico........................	576	734	12	253	649	16
New York............................	6,552	826	10	3,005	760	8
North Carolina.....................	2,954	687	13	1,373	630	11
North Dakota.......................	249	718	14	109	621	12
Ohio...................................	3,674	742	8	1,602	669	13
Oklahoma...........................	1,237	677	15	534	601	13
Oregon...............................	1,167	774	19	511	701	16
Pennsylvania.......................	4,242	760	8	1,858	680	12
Rhode Island.......................	343	830	21	159	746	27
South Carolina.....................	1,396	650	15	660	585	13
South Dakota.......................	286	660	12	133	602	9
Tennessee..........................	2,059	655	13	919	605	12
Texas.................................	8,634	680	7	3,694	619	8
Utah..................................	880	718	11	336	615	13
Vermont..............................	221	753	12	99	704	17
Virginia...............................	2,926	831	19	1,317	745	16
Washington.........................	2,126	877	21	877	743	18
West Virginia.......................	559	695	15	242	595	13
Wisconsin...........................	1,873	763	13	840	693	23
Wyoming.............................	201	788	16	79	638	17

Table 3. Median usual weekly earnings of full-time wage and salary workers, by state and sex, 2011 annual averages—cont'd

State	Men			Women's earnings as a percent of men's
	Number of workers (in thousands)	Median weekly earnings	Standard error of median	
United States..............................	55,971	$832	$3	82.2
Alabama................................	801	753	19	79.0
Alaska..................................	144	967	24	75.5
Arizona.................................	1,117	784	21	88.5
Arkansas...............................	504	675	20	84.0
California..............................	6,367	835	15	89.9
Colorado...............................	1,008	930	20	79.6
Connecticut............................	671	1,106	49	79.4
Delaware...............................	165	844	29	85.2
District of Columbia.....................	126	1,151	22	82.5
Florida.................................	3,172	797	14	83.8
Georgia................................	1,746	800	19	80.1
Hawaii.................................	221	842	29	78.0
Idaho..................................	271	769	19	78.5
Illinois................................	2,415	889	18	77.7
Indiana................................	1,244	799	24	76.0
Iowa...................................	591	799	22	82.1
Kansas.................................	566	811	20	78.9
Kentucky...............................	735	747	14	82.1
Louisiana..............................	790	862	33	68.7
Maine..................................	227	795	24	80.0
Maryland...............................	1,132	963	27	84.6
Massachusetts..........................	1,231	1,058	19	80.6
Michigan...............................	1,605	867	22	79.0
Minnesota..............................	1,042	921	21	80.7
Mississippi.............................	469	716	25	81.3
Missouri................................	1,081	841	20	74.7
Montana................................	153	725	21	77.8
Nebraska...............................	358	755	19	83.6
Nevada................................	477	735	15	88.4
New Hampshire.........................	269	977	25	76.6
New Jersey.............................	1,717	997	22	83.4
New Mexico.............................	323	774	18	83.9
New York...............................	3,547	894	15	85.0
North Carolina..........................	1,581	751	14	83.9
North Dakota...........................	140	810	25	76.7
Ohio...................................	2,072	800	14	83.6
Oklahoma..............................	703	765	16	78.6
Oregon................................	656	877	23	79.9
Pennsylvania...........................	2,384	833	15	81.6
Rhode Island...........................	183	917	30	81.4
South Carolina..........................	736	742	23	78.8
South Dakota...........................	152	730	16	82.5
Tennessee.............................	1,140	712	19	85.0
Texas..................................	4,940	730	9	84.8
Utah...................................	544	847	32	72.6
Vermont................................	122	819	29	86.0
Virginia................................	1,610	925	25	80.5
Washington.............................	1,249	997	21	74.5
West Virginia...........................	317	797	26	74.7
Wisconsin..............................	1,033	829	23	83.6
Wyoming...............................	122	915	20	69.7

NOTE: In general, the sampling error for the state estimates is considerably larger than it is for the national estimates; thus, comparisons of state estimates should be made with caution.

SOURCE: U.S. Bureau of Labor Statistics.

Table 4. **Median usual weekly earnings of part-time wage and salary workers, by selected characteristics, 2011 annual averages**

Characteristic	Both sexes			Women		
	Number of workers (in thousands)	Median weekly earnings	Standard error of median	Number of workers (in thousands)	Median weekly earnings	Standard error of median
Age						
Total, 16 years and older........................	24,502	$232	$1	15,903	$235	$2
16 to 24 years...	8,151	173	1	4,481	170	2
16 to 19 years.....................................	3,265	140	2	1,792	136	3
20 to 24 years.....................................	4,886	199	2	2,689	197	3
25 years and older..................................	16,352	273	2	11,422	271	2
25 to 34 years.....................................	4,337	263	3	2,804	260	4
35 to 44 years.....................................	3,399	296	4	2,591	294	5
45 to 54 years.....................................	3,510	291	4	2,695	286	5
55 to 64 years.....................................	3,077	280	5	2,229	277	5
65 years and older...............................	2,027	227	5	1,102	210	6
Race and Hispanic or Latino Ethnicity						
White...	20,233	233	1	13,280	237	2
Black or African American.......................	2,626	220	3	1,607	220	4
Asian...	950	255	6	595	254	8
Hispanic or Latino ethnicity....................	3,560	229	3	2,038	222	3
Marital Status						
Never married...	11,199	193	1	6,074	190	2
Married, spouse present.........................	9,851	290	3	7,242	290	3
Other marital status................................	3,452	245	3	2,587	241	4
Divorced..	1,894	262	5	1,415	261	6
Separated..	866	238	6	575	231	7
Widowed...	692	216	6	596	212	7

See note at end of table.

Table 4. Median usual weekly earnings of part-time wage and salary workers, by selected characteristics, 2011 annual averages—cont'd

Characteristic	Men			Women's earnings as a percent of men's
	Number of workers (in thousands)	Median weekly earnings	Standard error of median	
Age				
Total, 16 years and older....................................	8,599	$223	$2	104.0
16 to 24 years...	3,670	177	2	96.0
16 to 19 years....................................	1,473	145	3	93.8
20 to 24 years....................................	2,197	201	3	98.0
25 years and older....................................	4,930	273	3	97.5
25 to 34 years....................................	1,533	263	4	97.0
35 to 44 years....................................	808	300	8	98.0
45 to 54 years....................................	815	305	8	93.8
55 to 64 years....................................	848	287	8	96.5
65 years and older....................................	925	243	7	84.7
Race and Hispanic or Latino Ethnicity				
White..	6,953	223	2	104.9
Black or African American..................................	1,018	220	5	100.0
Asian..	355	253	10	98.4
Hispanic or Latino ethnicity.................................	1,522	239	4	92.9
Marital Status				
Never married..	5,126	197	2	96.4
Married, spouse present....................................	2,609	292	4	99.3
Other marital status.......................................	865	257	6	93.8
Divorced...	479	265	9	98.5
Separated..	291	250	9	92.4
Widowed...	96	243	19	85.1

NOTE: Estimates for the race groups listed (White, Black or African American, and Asian) do not sum to totals because data are not presented for all races. Persons whose ethnicity is identified as Hispanic or Latino may be of any race.

SOURCE: U.S. Bureau of Labor Statistics.

Table 5. Median usual weekly earnings of wage and salary workers, by hours usually worked and sex, 2011 annual averages

Hours of work	Both sexes			Women		
	Number of workers (in thousands)	Median weekly earnings	Standard error of median	Number of workers (in thousands)	Median weekly earnings	Standard error of median
Total, 16 years and older..................................	125,187	$642	$2	60,502	$565	$3
1 to 34 hours..	21,989	236	1	14,371	241	2
1 to 4 hours...	564	62	3	374	61	3
5 to 9 hours...	1,219	74	2	790	76	3
10 to 14 hours...	1,881	113	1	1,241	114	1
15 to 19 hours...	2,666	157	2	1,726	159	2
20 to 24 hours...	6,381	215	1	4,226	222	2
25 to 29 hours...	3,105	264	2	2,008	268	3
30 to 34 hours...	6,173	342	3	4,006	351	4
35 or more hours..	95,423	761	2	42,571	691	3
35 to 39 hours...	8,185	494	5	5,457	510	5
40 hours...	67,749	712	2	31,096	666	3
41 or more hours.....................................	19,489	1,158	5	6,018	1,050	10
41 to 44 hours......................................	1,101	872	17	428	796	20
45 to 48 hours......................................	5,278	1,033	10	1,880	977	14
49 to 59 hours......................................	8,847	1,235	9	2,696	1,148	12
60 or more hours..................................	4,263	1,313	24	1,015	1,160	19
Hours vary..	7,775	405	6	3,560	302	6
Usually less than 35 hours......................	2,513	192	4	1,532	188	4
Usually 35 or more hours........................	5,034	612	9	1,915	467	12

See note at end of table.

Table 5. **Median usual weekly earnings of wage and salary workers, by hours usually worked and sex, 2011 annual averages—cont'd**

Hours of work	Men			Women's earnings as a percent of men's
	Number of workers (in thousands)	Median weekly earnings	Standard error of median	
Total, 16 years and older....................................	64,686	$741	$3	76.2
1 to 34 hours..	7,618	229	2	105.2
1 to 4 hours..	191	63	5	96.8
5 to 9 hours..	429	71	2	107.0
10 to 14 hours..	640	112	2	101.8
15 to 19 hours..	940	155	3	102.6
20 to 24 hours..	2,155	203	2	109.4
25 to 29 hours..	1,098	255	4	105.1
30 to 34 hours..	2,167	324	4	108.3
35 or more hours..	52,852	833	4	82.5
35 to 39 hours..	2,728	464	7	109.9
40 hours..	36,653	753	3	88.4
41 or more hours..	13,471	1,210	10	86.8
41 to 44 hours..	674	924	27	86.1
45 to 48 hours..	3,398	1,073	15	91.1
49 to 59 hours..	6,151	1,263	14	90.5
60 or more hours..	3,247	1,351	18	85.9
Hours vary..	4,216	540	15	55.9
Usually less than 35 hours......................	981	199	6	94.5
Usually 35 or more hours.......................	3,119	716	14	65.2

NOTE: Data refer to the sole or principal job of full-time and part-time workers. Estimates for the "hours vary" groups do not sum to totals because data are not presented for a small number of multiple jobholders whose usual number of hours on the principal job is not identifiable.

SOURCE: U.S. Bureau of Labor Statistics.

Table 6. Quartiles and selected deciles of usual weekly earnings of full-time wage and salary workers, by selected characteristics, 2011 annual averages

Characteristic	Number of workers (in thousands)	Upper limit of:				
		First decile	First quartile	Second quartile (median)	Third quartile	Ninth decile
Sex, Race, and Hispanic or Latino Ethnicity						
Total, 16 years and older............................	100,457	$358	$499	$756	$1,173	$1,802
Women...	44,486	340	470	684	1,023	1,515
Men...	55,971	378	529	832	1,317	1,924
White...	81,336	365	510	775	1,205	1,846
Women...	34,976	345	480	703	1,050	1,537
Men...	46,360	382	548	856	1,345	1,985
Black or African American..........................	11,604	326	423	615	923	1,363
Women...	6,191	317	411	595	860	1,264
Men...	5,414	338	446	653	980	1,436
Asian...	5,197	378	534	866	1,411	2,023
Women...	2,284	354	498	751	1,184	1,769
Men...	2,912	395	592	970	1,586	2,294
Hispanic or Latino ethnicity........................	15,147	307	388	549	841	1,270
Women...	5,700	296	373	518	773	1,157
Men...	9,448	314	397	571	887	1,351
Educational Attainment						
Total, 25 years and older............................	91,733	380	528	797	1,228	1,867
Less than a high school diploma.............	7,019	288	346	451	616	862
High school graduates, no college..........	25,157	349	464	638	919	1,266
Some college or associate's degree........	25,205	387	519	739	1,063	1,476
Bachelor's degree and higher.................	34,353	571	783	1,150	1,743	2,475
Women, 25 years and older........................	40,714	358	493	718	1,070	1,556
Less than a high school diploma.............	2,225	269	316	395	516	677
High school graduates, no college..........	10,220	322	409	554	748	1,015
Some college or associate's degree........	12,048	360	479	645	913	1,237
Bachelor's degree and higher.................	16,221	524	726	998	1,443	2,001
Men, 25 years and older............................	51,020	399	581	886	1,371	2,009
Less than a high school diploma.............	4,794	299	368	488	674	950
High school graduates, no college..........	14,937	381	508	720	1,023	1,419
Some college or associate's degree........	13,156	420	589	840	1,195	1,645
Bachelor's degree and higher.................	18,132	607	888	1,332	1,913	2,882

NOTE: Ten percent of all full-time wage and salary workers earn less than the upper limit of the first decile; 25 percent earn less than the upper limit of the first quartile; 50 percent earn less than the upper limit of the second quartile, or median; 75 percent earn less than the upper limit of the third quartile; and 90 percent earn less than the upper limit of the ninth decile. Estimates for the race groups listed (White, Black or African American, and Asian) do not sum to totals because data are not presented for all races. Persons whose ethnicity is identified as Hispanic or Latino may be of any race.

SOURCE: U.S. Bureau of Labor Statistics.

Table 7. Distribution of full-time wage and salary workers, by usual weekly earnings and selected characteristics, 2011 annual averages

(In thousands)

Characteristic	Total employed	Number of workers by usual weekly earnings							
		Under $150.00	$150.00 to $249.99	$250.00 to $349.99	$350.00 to $499.99	$500.00 to $749.99	$750.00 to $999.99	$1,000.00 to $1,499.00	$1,500.00 or more
Age and Sex									
Total, 16 years and older..........	100,457	805	1,261	6,676	16,119	23,643	17,420	18,771	15,761
16 to 24 years......................	8,723	169	290	1,815	2,990	2,121	786	408	143
16 to 19 years...................	947	52	62	330	312	132	41	13	5
20 to 24 years...................	7,776	117	229	1,485	2,678	1,989	745	395	138
25 years and older...............	91,733	636	971	4,860	13,129	21,523	16,633	18,363	15,618
25 to 34 years...................	24,296	156	268	1,659	4,522	6,690	4,640	4,135	2,226
35 to 44 years...................	23,782	139	222	1,152	3,186	5,313	4,224	4,885	4,662
45 to 54 years...................	25,133	174	228	1,196	3,145	5,391	4,517	5,395	5,087
55 to 64 years...................	15,641	103	169	670	1,846	3,450	2,788	3,472	3,145
65 years and older............	2,881	63	84	183	430	679	465	478	498
Women, 16 years and older.....	44,486	448	695	3,585	8,105	11,687	7,960	7,332	4,673
16 to 24 years......................	3,772	84	137	913	1,269	878	336	108	47
16 to 19 years...................	389	32	33	148	116	37	17	3	3
20 to 24 years...................	3,383	52	105	765	1,154	840	319	104	44
25 years and older...............	40,714	364	557	2,672	6,836	10,809	7,624	7,225	4,626
25 to 34 years...................	10,392	80	142	799	2,000	3,029	2,080	1,572	690
35 to 44 years...................	10,204	86	119	655	1,707	2,597	1,843	1,846	1,352
45 to 54 years...................	11,557	110	140	724	1,808	2,938	2,104	2,162	1,572
55 to 64 years...................	7,294	60	108	392	1,089	1,927	1,358	1,445	914
65 years and older............	1,266	29	48	102	233	317	239	200	97
Men, 16 years and older...........	55,971	357	566	3,090	8,014	11,957	9,460	11,439	11,088
16 to 24 years......................	4,951	85	153	902	1,721	1,243	450	300	96
16 to 19 years...................	558	20	29	182	197	95	24	10	1
20 to 24 years...................	4,393	65	124	720	1,524	1,148	426	290	94
25 years and older...............	51,020	271	413	2,188	6,293	10,714	9,010	11,139	10,992
25 to 34 years...................	13,905	77	126	860	2,523	3,661	2,559	2,563	1,537
35 to 44 years...................	13,578	54	102	496	1,479	2,716	2,381	3,039	3,310
45 to 54 years...................	13,576	64	89	472	1,337	2,453	2,414	3,233	3,514
55 to 64 years...................	8,347	43	61	278	757	1,522	1,430	2,027	2,230
65 years and older............	1,614	34	36	82	197	361	226	278	401

See note at end of table.

Table 7. **Distribution of full-time wage and salary workers, by usual weekly earnings and selected characteristics, 2011 annual averages—cont'd**

(In thousands)

Characteristic	Total employed	Number of workers by usual weekly earnings							
		Under $150.00	$150.00 to $249.99	$250.00 to $349.99	$350.00 to $499.99	$500.00 to $749.99	$750.00 to $999.99	$1,000.00 to $1,499.00	$1,500.00 or more
Race, Hispanic or Latino Ethnicity, and Sex									
White..................................	81,336	647	952	5,071	12,340	18,842	14,293	15,786	13,406
Women..............................	34,976	355	515	2,655	6,091	9,092	6,401	6,035	3,833
Men...................................	46,360	293	436	2,417	6,248	9,750	7,892	9,751	9,573
Black or African American......	11,604	102	217	1,100	2,614	3,171	1,925	1,566	910
Women..............................	6,191	61	132	657	1,444	1,747	1,010	729	412
Men...................................	5,414	41	85	443	1,170	1,424	915	837	499
Asian.................................	5,197	32	58	298	720	1,024	846	1,047	1,171
Women..............................	2,284	20	28	167	358	540	390	429	353
Men...................................	2,912	12	31	132	362	484	456	618	818
Hispanic or Latino ethnicity...	15,147	134	324	2,057	3,971	3,880	2,033	1,727	1,021
Women..............................	5,700	68	159	902	1,532	1,465	732	566	275
Men...................................	9,448	66	165	1,155	2,438	2,415	1,301	1,161	746

NOTE: Estimates for the race groups listed (White, Black or African American, and Asian) do not sum to totals because data are not presented for all races. Persons whose ethnicity is identified as Hispanic or Latino may be of any race.

SOURCE: U.S. Bureau of Labor Statistics.

Table 8. **Median usual weekly earnings of full-time wage and salary workers, by sex, marital status, and presence and age of own children under 18 years old, 2011 annual averages**

Characteristic	Number of workers (in thousands)	Median weekly earnings	Standard error of median
Women			
Total, all marital statuses...	44,486	$684	$3
With children under 18 years.......................................	16,093	669	4
With children 6 to 17 years, none younger..................	9,714	687	6
With children under 6 years..	6,379	644	6
With no children under 18 years..................................	28,393	692	3
Total, married, spouse present.......................................	23,274	741	3
With children under 18 years.......................................	10,622	743	4
With children 6 to 17 years, none younger..................	6,330	737	6
With children under 6 years..	4,293	752	7
With no children under 18 years..................................	12,651	740	4
Total, other marital statuses[1].......................................	21,212	620	3
With children under 18 years.......................................	5,471	563	6
With children 6 to 17 years, none younger..................	3,384	608	5
With children under 6 years..	2,086	494	5
With no children under 18 years..................................	15,741	649	4
Men			
Total, all marital statuses...	55,971	832	3
With children under 18 years.......................................	20,808	919	6
With children 6 to 17 years, none younger..................	10,990	972	7
With children under 6 years..	9,818	847	9
With no children under 18 years..................................	35,163	784	4
Total, married, spouse present.......................................	33,777	955	4
With children under 18 years.......................................	18,462	959	6
With children 6 to 17 years, none younger..................	9,881	998	8
With children under 6 years..	8,581	907	9
With no children under 18 years..................................	15,314	952	6
Total, other marital statuses[1].......................................	22,194	674	4
With children under 18 years.......................................	2,346	656	12
With children 6 to 17 years, none younger..................	1,109	778	17
With children under 6 years..	1,237	577	10
With no children under 18 years..................................	19,848	676	4

[1] Includes never-married, divorced, separated, and widowed persons.

NOTE: Children refer to "own" children and include sons, daughters, stepchildren, and adopted children. Excluded are other related children such as grandchildren, nieces, nephews, and cousins, as well as unrelated children.

SOURCE: U.S. Bureau of Labor Statistics.

Table 9. Median hourly earnings of wage and salary workers paid hourly rates, by selected characteristics, 2011 annual averages

Characteristic	Both sexes			Women		
	Number of workers (in thousands)	Median weekly earnings	Standard error of median	Number of workers (in thousands)	Median weekly earnings	Standard error of median
Age						
Total, 16 years and older....................	73,926	$12.71	$0.04	37,469	$11.98	$0.03
16 to 24 years.................................	14,436	8.97	.02	7,147	8.73	.03
16 to 19 years............................	3,936	8.06	.02	2,064	7.96	.03
20 to 24 years............................	10,501	9.61	.06	5,083	9.16	.03
25 years and older...........................	59,490	14.12	.03	30,323	13.10	.04
25 to 34 years............................	17,155	12.71	.07	8,024	12.12	.05
35 to 44 years............................	14,168	14.83	.05	7,132	13.44	.14
45 to 54 years............................	15,331	15.00	.04	8,164	13.76	.10
55 to 64 years............................	10,046	15.07	.05	5,555	14.03	.09
65 years and older......................	2,790	12.19	.09	1,448	11.76	.20
Race and Hispanic or Latino Ethnicity						
White..	59,314	12.91	.03	29,571	12.05	.03
Black or African American..................	9,523	11.79	.07	5,271	11.28	.11
Asian..	3,037	13.35	.22	1,612	12.80	.21
Hispanic or Latino ethnicity...............	13,264	11.05	.06	5,561	10.25	.08
Marital Status						
Never married....................................	26,703	10.12	.02	12,571	9.86	.03
Married, spouse present.....................	34,624	14.91	.03	17,162	13.78	.07
Other marital status...........................	12,599	13.18	.08	7,736	12.28	.08
Divorced..	7,933	14.14	.09	4,792	13.01	.10
Separated......................................	3,171	11.85	.08	1,749	11.17	.18
Widowed..	1,496	12.15	.14	1,194	11.79	.18
Union Affiliation[1]						
Members of unions[2]..........................	8,869	18.32	.18	3,497	16.00	.14
Represented by unions[3].....................	9,681	18.12	.11	3,923	15.87	.15
Not represented by a union................	64,245	12.07	.02	33,546	11.69	.05
Educational Attainment						
Total, 25 years and older....................	59,490	14.12	.03	30,323	13.10	.04
Less than a high school diploma.........	6,905	10.20	.03	2,706	9.22	.05
High school graduates, no college......	21,386	13.46	.08	10,002	11.97	.04
Some college or associate's degree....	19,562	14.78	.06	10,694	13.70	.09
Bachelor's degree and higher.............	11,637	18.59	.19	6,920	18.06	.10

See footnotes at end of table.

Table 9. Median hourly earnings of wage and salary workers paid hourly rates, by selected characteristics, 2011 annual averages—cont'd

Characteristic	Men			Women's earnings as a percent of men's
	Number of workers (in thousands)	Median weekly earnings	Standard error of median	
Age				
Total, 16 years and older...............................	36,457	$13.80	$0.06	86.8
16 to 24 years...	7,290	9.23	.05	94.6
16 to 19 years...	1,872	8.16	.03	97.5
20 to 24 years...	5,418	9.90	.03	92.5
25 years and older..	29,167	15.11	.03	86.7
25 to 34 years...	9,132	13.18	.09	92.0
35 to 44 years...	7,036	16.03	.10	83.8
45 to 54 years...	7,167	16.88	.13	81.5
55 to 64 years...	4,491	17.07	.21	82.2
65 years and older...................................	1,341	12.85	.17	91.5
Race and Hispanic or Latino Ethnicity				
White...	29,743	14.02	.04	85.9
Black or African American.............................	4,252	12.06	.06	93.5
Asian...	1,425	14.25	.48	89.8
Hispanic or Latino ethnicity..........................	7,703	11.81	.08	86.8
Marital Status				
Never married..	14,132	10.52	.09	93.7
Married, spouse present................................	17,462	16.05	.06	85.9
Other marital status......................................	4,864	14.90	.07	82.4
Divorced...	3,140	15.77	.21	82.5
Separated...	1,422	12.36	.28	90.4
Widowed...	302	15.02	.25	78.5
Union Affiliation[1]				
Members of unions[2].....................................	5,372	20.04	.08	79.8
Represented by unions[3]..............................	5,758	19.95	.08	79.5
Not represented by a union............................	30,699	12.76	.06	91.6
Educational Attainment				
Total, 25 years and older...............................	29,167	15.11	.03	86.7
Less than a high school diploma.....................	4,199	11.10	.08	83.1
High school graduates, no college...................	11,383	15.03	.04	79.6
Some college or associate's degree.................	8,868	16.08	.09	85.2
Bachelor's degree and higher.........................	4,717	19.43	.28	92.9

[1] Differences in earnings levels between workers with and without union affiliation reflect a variety of factors in addition to coverage by a collective bargaining agreement, including the distribution of male and female employees by occupation, industry, firm size, and geographic region.

[2] Data refer to members of a labor union or an employee association similar to a union.

[3] Data refer to workers who report no union affiliation but whose jobs are covered by a union or an employee association contract, as well as to members of a labor union or an employee association similar to a union.

NOTE: Workers paid hourly rates represented 59 percent of all wage and salary workers in 2011. Estimates for the race groups listed (White, Black or African American, and Asian) do not sum to totals because data are not presented for all races. Persons whose ethnicity is identified as Hispanic or Latino may be of any race.

SOURCE: U.S. Bureau of Labor Statistics.

Table 10. **Distribution of wage and salary workers paid hourly rates, by hourly earnings and selected characteristics, 2011 annual averages**

(In thousands)

Characteristic	Total employed	Number of workers by hourly earnings						
		Under $6.00	$6.00 to $7.99	$8.00 to $9.99	$10.00 to $11.99	$12.00 to $14.99	$15.00 to $19.99	$20.00 or more
Age and sex								
Total, 16 years and older............	73,926	1,250	5,559	13,752	11,535	12,591	13,245	15,993
16 to 24 years........................	14,436	533	2,914	5,223	2,685	1,657	989	436
16 to 19 years.....................	3,936	178	1,451	1,586	430	188	72	30
20 to 24 years.....................	10,501	354	1,463	3,638	2,254	1,469	917	406
25 years and older.................	59,490	717	2,645	8,529	8,851	10,934	12,256	15,558
25 to 34 years.....................	17,155	366	953	2,975	2,934	3,484	3,356	3,088
35 to 44 years.....................	14,168	143	519	1,886	2,006	2,490	2,970	4,154
45 to 54 years.....................	15,331	140	586	1,943	2,039	2,680	3,298	4,645
55 to 64 years.....................	10,046	45	380	1,215	1,364	1,747	2,180	3,115
65 years and older.............	2,790	24	208	511	507	532	453	555
Women, 16 years and older.......	37,469	867	3,312	7,758	6,103	6,593	6,124	6,713
16 to 24 years........................	7,147	365	1,605	2,722	1,169	755	353	177
16 to 19 years.....................	2,064	130	804	825	204	67	22	12
20 to 24 years.....................	5,083	236	801	1,897	965	688	330	166
25 years and older.................	30,323	501	1,707	5,036	4,934	5,838	5,772	6,535
25 to 34 years.....................	8,024	246	592	1,498	1,370	1,620	1,355	1,342
35 to 44 years.....................	7,132	97	353	1,142	1,137	1,368	1,329	1,706
45 to 54 years.....................	8,164	110	388	1,295	1,259	1,540	1,662	1,910
55 to 64 years.....................	5,555	33	253	796	879	1,054	1,227	1,312
65 years and older.............	1,448	16	121	304	289	256	197	265
Men, 16 years and older............	36,457	383	2,247	5,994	5,432	5,998	7,121	9,281
16 to 24 years........................	7,290	167	1,309	2,501	1,516	902	636	258
16 to 19 years.....................	1,872	49	647	761	226	121	49	18
20 to 24 years.....................	5,418	119	661	1,741	1,290	781	587	240
25 years and older.................	29,167	216	938	3,493	3,917	5,096	6,485	9,022
25 to 34 years.....................	9,132	120	361	1,476	1,564	1,864	2,000	1,746
35 to 44 years.....................	7,036	46	166	744	869	1,122	1,641	2,448
45 to 54 years.....................	7,167	30	198	648	780	1,140	1,636	2,736
55 to 64 years.....................	4,491	12	126	419	485	694	953	1,803
65 years and older.............	1,341	8	87	207	219	276	255	290

See note at end of table.

Table 10. **Distribution of wage and salary workers paid hourly rates, by hourly earnings and selected characteristics, 2011 annual averages—cont'd**

(In thousands)

Characteristic	Total employed	Number of workers by hourly earnings						
		Under $6.00	$6.00 to $7.99	$8.00 to $9.99	$10.00 to $11.99	$12.00 to $14.99	$15.00 to $19.99	$20.00 or more
Race, Hispanic or Latino Ethnicity, and Sex								
White.................................	59,314	1,073	4,279	10,834	8,959	9,957	10,830	13,382
Women..............................	29,571	755	2,541	6,010	4,721	5,143	4,901	5,500
Men..................................	29,743	317	1,738	4,824	4,238	4,815	5,929	7,882
Black or African American.......	9,523	92	944	1,971	1,763	1,817	1,468	1,469
Women..............................	5,271	54	577	1,205	963	999	757	716
Men..................................	4,252	37	367	765	800	817	711	754
Asian.................................	3,037	39	160	520	472	505	554	788
Women..............................	1,612	24	98	308	250	288	276	367
Men..................................	1,425	15	62	212	222	217	277	420
Hispanic or Latino ethnicity......	13,264	200	1,024	3,465	2,460	2,380	2,000	1,734
Women..............................	5,561	109	564	1,677	984	979	739	510
Men..................................	7,703	91	461	1,788	1,477	1,401	1,262	1,224

NOTE: Workers paid hourly rates represented 59 percent of all wage and salary workers in 2011. Estimates for the race groups listed (White, Black or African American, and Asian) do not sum to totals because data are not presented for all races. Persons whose ethnicity is identified as Hispanic or Latino may be of any race.

SOURCE: U.S. Bureau of Labor Statistics.

Table 11. Wage and salary workers paid hourly rates with earnings at or below the prevailing federal minimum wage, by selected characteristics, 2011 annual averages

(Numbers in thousands)

Characteristic	Workers paid hourly rates				
	Total	Below prevailing federal minimum wage	At prevailing federal minimum wage	Total at or below prevailing federal minimum wage	
				Number	Percent of workers paid hourly rates
Age and sex					
Total, 16 years and older...............................	73,926	2,152	1,677	3,829	5.2
16 to 24 years.......................................	14,436	1,003	893	1,896	13.1
16 to 19 years.................................	3,936	408	491	899	22.8
20 to 24 years.................................	10,501	595	402	997	9.5
25 years and older..............................	59,490	1,149	784	1,933	3.2
25 to 34 years.................................	17,155	509	299	808	4.7
35 to 44 years.................................	14,168	238	161	399	2.8
45 to 54 years.................................	15,331	223	159	382	2.5
55 to 64 years.................................	10,046	104	117	221	2.2
65 years and older............................	2,790	75	48	123	4.4
Women, 16 years and older........................	37,469	1,366	1,029	2,395	6.4
16 to 24 years.......................................	7,147	604	505	1,109	15.5
16 to 19 years.................................	2,064	247	279	526	25.5
20 to 24 years.................................	5,083	357	226	583	11.5
25 years and older..............................	30,323	762	524	1,286	4.2
25 to 34 years.................................	8,024	326	202	528	6.6
35 to 44 years.................................	7,132	152	105	257	3.6
45 to 54 years.................................	8,164	165	105	270	3.3
55 to 64 years.................................	5,555	69	81	150	2.7
65 years and older............................	1,448	50	31	81	5.6
Men, 16 years and older............................	36,457	785	648	1,433	3.9
16 to 24 years.......................................	7,290	399	388	787	10.8
16 to 19 years.................................	1,872	161	212	373	19.9
20 to 24 years.................................	5,418	238	175	413	7.6
25 years and older..............................	29,167	387	260	647	2.2
25 to 34 years.................................	9,132	182	96	278	3.0
35 to 44 years.................................	7,036	86	56	142	2.0
45 to 54 years.................................	7,167	58	55	113	1.6
55 to 64 years.................................	4,491	36	36	72	1.6
65 years and older............................	1,341	25	17	42	3.1

See note at end of table.

Table 11. **Wage and salary workers paid hourly rates with earnings at or below the prevailing federal minimum wage, by selected characteristics, 2011 annual averages—cont'd**

(Numbers in thousands)

Characteristic	Workers paid hourly rates				
	Total	Below prevailing federal minimum wage	At prevailing federal minimum wage	Total at or below prevailing federal minimum wage	
				Number	Percent of workers paid hourly rates
Race and Hispanic or Latino Ethnicity					
White..	59,314	1,748	1,258	3,006	5.1
Women..	29,571	1,124	774	1,898	6.4
Men..	29,743	624	484	1,108	3.7
Black or African American............................	9,523	253	324	577	6.1
Women..	5,271	148	208	356	6.8
Men..	4,252	105	117	221	5.2
Asian..	3,037	63	36	99	3.3
Women..	1,612	35	23	58	3.6
Men..	1,425	28	13	41	2.9
Hispanic or Latino ethnicity.........................	13,264	380	340	720	5.4
Women..	5,561	208	186	394	7.1
Men..	7,703	172	154	326	4.2
Full- and Part-time Status and Sex[1]					
Full-time workers.......................................	53,594	752	522	1,274	2.4
Women..	24,302	456	317	773	3.2
Men..	29,292	296	205	501	1.7
Part-time workers......................................	20,199	1,392	1,153	2,545	12.6
Women..	13,096	904	711	1,615	12.3
Men..	7,103	489	443	932	13.1

[1] The distinction between full-time and part-time workers is based on hours usually worked. These data do not sum to totals because full-time or part-time status on the principal or main job is not identifiable for a small number of multiple jobholders.

NOTE: The prevailing federal minimum wage was $7.25 in 2011. See the technical note for more information about minimum wage workers. Estimates for the race groups listed (White, Black or African American, and Asian) do not sum to totals because data are not presented for all races. Persons whose ethnicity is identified as Hispanic or Latino may be of any race.

SOURCE: U.S. Bureau of Labor Statistics.

Table 12. **Wage and salary workers paid hourly rates with earnings at or below the prevailing federal minimum wage, by sex, 1979–2011 annual averages**

(Numbers in thousands)

Year and sex	Total wage and salary workers	Workers paid hourly rates						
		Total	Percent of total wage and salary workers	Below prevailing federal minimum wage	At prevailing federal minimum wage	Total at or below prevailing federal minimum wage	
						Number	Percent of workers paid hourly rates
Both Sexes							
1979...............................	87,529	51,721	59.1	2,916	3,997	6,912	13.4
1980...............................	87,644	51,335	58.6	3,087	4,686	7,773	15.1
1981...............................	88,516	51,869	58.6	3,513	4,311	7,824	15.1
1982...............................	87,368	50,846	58.2	2,348	4,148	6,496	12.8
1983...............................	88,290	51,820	58.7	2,077	4,261	6,338	12.2
1984...............................	92,194	54,143	58.7	1,838	4,125	5,963	11.0
1985...............................	94,521	55,762	59.0	1,639	3,899	5,538	9.9
1986...............................	96,903	57,529	59.4	1,599	3,461	5,060	8.8
1987...............................	99,303	59,552	60.0	1,468	3,229	4,698	7.9
1988...............................	101,407	60,878	60.0	1,319	2,608	3,927	6.5
1989...............................	103,480	62,389	60.3	1,372	1,790	3,162	5.1
1990...............................	104,876	63,172	60.2	[1]2,132	[1]1,096	[1]3,228	[1]5.1
1991...............................	103,723	62,627	60.4	[1]2,377	[1]2,906	[1]5,283	[1]8.4
1992...............................	104,668	63,610	60.8	1,939	2,982	4,921	7.7
1993...............................	106,101	64,274	60.6	1,707	2,625	4,332	6.7
1994...............................	107,989	66,549	61.6	1,995	2,132	4,128	6.2
1995...............................	110,038	68,354	62.1	1,699	1,956	3,656	5.3
1996...............................	111,960	69,255	61.9	[1]1,863	[1]1,861	[1]3,724	[1]5.4
1997...............................	114,533	70,735	61.8	[1]2,990	[1]1,764	[1]4,754	[1]6.7
1998...............................	116,730	71,440	61.2	2,834	1,593	4,427	6.2
1999...............................	118,963	72,306	60.8	2,194	1,146	3,340	4.6
2000...............................	122,089	73,496	60.2	1,752	898	2,650	3.6
2001...............................	122,229	73,392	60.0	1,518	656	2,174	3.0
2002...............................	121,826	72,508	59.5	1,579	567	2,146	3.0
2003...............................	122,358	72,946	59.6	1,555	545	2,100	2.9
2004...............................	123,554	73,939	59.8	1,483	520	2,003	2.7
2005...............................	125,889	75,609	60.1	1,403	479	1,882	2.5
2006...............................	128,237	76,514	59.7	1,283	409	1,692	2.2
2007...............................	129,767	75,873	58.5	[1]1,462	[1]267	[1]1,729	[1]2.3
2008...............................	129,377	75,305	58.2	[1]1,940	[1]286	[1]2,226	[1]3.0
2009...............................	124,490	72,611	58.3	[1]2,592	[1]980	[1]3,572	[1]4.9
2010...............................	124,073	72,902	58.8	2,541	1,820	4,361	6.0
2011...............................	125,187	73,926	59.1	2,152	1,677	3,829	5.2

See footnote at end of table.

Table 12. **Wage and salary workers paid hourly rates with earnings at or below the prevailing federal minimum wage, by sex, 1979–2011 annual averages—cont'd**

(Numbers in thousands)

Year and sex	Total wage and salary workers	Workers paid hourly rates					
		Total	Percent of total wage and salary workers	Below prevailing federal minimum wage	At prevailing federal minimum wage	Total at or below prevailing federal minimum wage	
						Number	Percent of workers paid hourly rates
Women							
1979	38,129	23,329	61.2	2,070	2,644	4,714	20.2
1980	38,944	23,626	60.7	2,104	2,990	5,095	21.6
1981	39,672	24,294	61.2	2,394	2,778	5,172	21.3
1982	39,777	24,365	61.3	1,651	2,561	4,212	17.3
1983	40,433	24,989	61.8	1,492	2,603	4,095	16.4
1984	42,172	26,003	61.7	1,348	2,499	3,847	14.8
1985	43,506	26,869	61.8	1,198	2,356	3,554	13.2
1986	44,961	27,863	62.0	1,192	2,125	3,317	11.9
1987	46,365	29,078	62.7	1,105	1,946	3,051	10.5
1988	47,495	29,820	62.8	1,008	1,542	2,550	8.6
1989	48,691	30,702	63.1	994	1,056	2,050	6.7
1990	49,323	31,069	63.0	[1]1,420	[1]711	[1]2,131	[1]6.9
1991	49,105	30,988	63.1	[1]1,582	[1]1,792	[1]3,374	[1]10.9
1992	49,842	31,454	63.1	1,286	1,751	3,036	9.7
1993	50,626	31,937	63.1	1,133	1,534	2,667	8.4
1994	51,419	33,021	64.2	1,322	1,241	2,563	7.8
1995	52,369	33,934	64.8	1,157	1,161	2,318	6.8
1996	53,488	34,418	64.3	[1]1,244	[1]1,106	[1]2,350	[1]6.8
1997	54,708	35,214	64.4	[1]1,843	[1]1,092	[1]2,935	[1]8.3
1998	55,757	35,680	64.0	1,794	965	2,760	7.7
1999	57,050	36,233	63.5	1,426	700	2,126	5.9
2000	58,427	36,777	62.9	1,170	579	1,749	4.8
2001	58,582	36,848	62.9	1,021	409	1,430	3.9
2002	58,555	36,508	62.3	997	350	1,347	3.7
2003	59,122	37,093	62.7	1,062	332	1,394	3.8
2004	59,408	37,133	62.5	1,013	310	1,323	3.6
2005	60,423	37,957	62.8	944	290	1,234	3.3
2006	61,426	38,321	62.4	861	263	1,124	2.9
2007	62,299	38,082	61.1	[1]1,002	[1]181	[1]1,183	[1]3.1
2008	62,532	37,972	60.7	[1]1,302	[1]196	[1]1,498	[1]3.9
2009	60,951	37,426	61.4	[1]1,603	[1]612	[1]2,215	[1]5.9
2010	60,542	37,404	61.8	1,598	1,151	2,749	7.3
2011	60,502	37,469	61.9	1,366	1,029	2,395	6.4

See footnote at end of table.

Table 12. **Wage and salary workers paid hourly rates with earnings at or below the prevailing federal minimum wage, by sex, 1979–2011 annual averages—cont'd**

(Numbers in thousands)

Year and sex	Total wage and salary workers	Workers paid hourly rates					
		Total	Percent of total wage and salary workers	Below prevailing federal minimum wage	At prevailing federal minimum wage	Total at or below prevailing federal minimum wage	
						Number	Percent of workers paid hourly rates
Men							
1979....................	49,400	28,392	57.5	846	1,353	2,199	7.7
1980....................	48,700	27,709	56.9	983	1,696	2,678	9.7
1981....................	48,844	27,576	56.5	1,119	1,533	2,652	9.6
1982....................	47,591	26,481	55.6	697	1,587	2,284	8.6
1983....................	47,856	26,831	56.1	585	1,658	2,243	8.4
1984....................	50,022	28,140	56.3	490	1,626	2,116	7.5
1985....................	51,015	28,893	56.6	440	1,544	1,984	6.9
1986....................	51,942	29,666	57.1	408	1,336	1,743	5.9
1987....................	52,938	30,474	57.6	364	1,283	1,647	5.4
1988....................	53,912	31,058	57.6	311	1,066	1,377	4.4
1989....................	54,789	31,687	57.8	379	733	1,112	3.5
1990....................	55,553	32,104	57.8	[1]712	[1]385	[1]1,097	[1]3.4
1991....................	54,618	31,639	57.9	[1]795	[1]1,114	[1]1,909	[1]6.0
1992....................	54,826	32,155	58.6	653	1,231	1,885	5.9
1993....................	55,475	32,337	58.3	573	1,091	1,664	5.1
1994....................	56,570	33,528	59.3	674	891	1,565	4.7
1995....................	57,669	34,420	59.7	542	796	1,338	3.9
1996....................	58,473	34,838	59.6	[1]619	[1]755	[1]1,374	[1]3.9
1997....................	59,825	35,521	59.4	[1]1,147	[1]673	[1]1,820	[1]5.1
1998....................	60,973	35,761	58.7	1,039	628	1,667	4.7
1999....................	61,914	36,073	58.3	768	446	1,214	3.4
2000....................	63,662	36,720	57.7	582	319	901	2.5
2001....................	63,647	36,544	57.4	497	247	744	2.0
2002....................	63,272	36,000	56.9	582	217	799	2.2
2003....................	63,236	35,853	56.7	493	213	706	2.0
2004....................	64,145	36,806	57.4	470	210	680	1.8
2005....................	65,466	37,652	57.5	459	189	648	1.7
2006....................	66,811	38,193	57.2	422	146	568	1.5
2007....................	67,468	37,790	56.0	[1]460	[1]86	[1]546	[1]1.4
2008....................	66,846	37,334	55.9	[1]638	[1]90	[1]728	[1]1.9
2009....................	63,539	35,185	55.4	[1]990	[1]368	[1]1,358	[1]3.9
2010....................	63,531	35,498	55.9	943	669	1,612	4.5
2011....................	64,686	36,457	56.4	785	648	1,433	3.9

[1] Data for 1990–91, 1996–97, and 2007–09 reflect changes in the minimum wage that took place in those years.

NOTE: The comparability of historical labor force data has been affected at various times by methodological and other changes in the Current Population Survey (CPS). Information about historical comparability is online at **www.bls.gov/cps/documentation.htm#comp.** The prevailing federal minimum wage was $2.90 in 1979, $3.10 in 1980, and $3.35 in 1981–89. The minimum wage rose to $3.80 in April 1990, to $4.25 in April 1991, to $4.75 in October 1996, to $5.15 in September 1997, to $5.85 in July 2007, to $6.55 in July 2008, and to $7.25 in July 2009. See the technical note for more information about minimum wage workers.

SOURCE: U.S. Bureau of Labor Statistics.

Table 13. Women's earnings as a percent of men's, by age, for full-time wage and salary workers, 1979–2011

Year	Total, 16 years and older	16 to 24 years			25 years and older					
		Total	16 to 19 years	20 to 24 years	Total	25 to 34 years	35 to 44 years	45 to 54 years	55 to 64 years	65 years and older
1979...............	62.3	78.6	85.2	76.3	62.1	67.5	58.3	56.8	60.6	77.6
1980...............	64.2	80.3	89.5	78.1	62.8	69.4	58.3	56.9	59.4	76.4
1981...............	64.4	82.6	91.7	80.6	62.6	70.3	59.9	56.8	58.9	71.1
1982...............	65.7	85.3	92.9	82.4	64.9	72.1	61.1	60.1	61.4	70.3
1983...............	66.5	88.8	94.0	85.5	65.8	73.3	61.5	59.5	61.8	68.8
1984...............	67.6	87.9	93.1	85.2	67.1	74.6	62.0	59.4	61.5	66.8
1985...............	68.1	87.6	90.7	85.7	66.8	75.1	63.0	59.7	61.0	65.9
1986...............	69.5	89.0	91.4	87.5	66.5	76.1	63.9	60.9	61.2	71.5
1987...............	69.8	88.3	87.8	88.0	67.3	76.7	66.1	62.3	62.2	68.7
1988...............	70.2	89.7	89.8	90.0	68.8	77.7	68.5	61.7	62.3	70.9
1989...............	70.1	90.8	94.3	89.7	70.2	78.3	68.3	62.7	63.9	74.3
1990...............	71.9	90.1	90.8	90.3	72.1	79.3	69.6	63.8	63.7	74.4
1991...............	74.2	93.3	93.6	93.3	74.0	81.0	70.7	65.0	64.5	68.3
1992...............	75.8	94.0	94.0	94.3	74.6	82.0	71.9	65.8	64.9	77.9
1993...............	77.1	94.8	92.8	95.4	74.8	83.0	73.0	67.4	67.4	74.3
1994...............	76.4	93.9	92.5	94.5	73.1	82.9	72.6	67.1	66.0	76.2
1995...............	75.5	90.8	88.1	92.4	72.8	82.2	72.6	67.7	64.7	80.0
1996...............	75.0	92.5	88.8	92.8	74.1	83.2	73.3	68.9	65.3	70.0
1997...............	74.4	92.1	91.6	90.5	75.1	82.9	74.0	69.4	64.7	77.0
1998...............	76.3	91.3	88.6	89.4	75.9	82.9	73.6	70.5	68.1	72.6
1999...............	76.5	91.0	91.4	90.5	74.4	81.5	71.7	70.0	67.9	78.7
2000...............	76.9	91.7	92.5	92.7	74.5	82.4	71.6	73.2	69.1	75.1
2001...............	76.4	90.3	90.3	91.9	75.4	83.0	72.5	73.5	70.5	69.0
2002...............	77.9	93.9	94.6	93.9	77.6	84.5	75.2	74.6	71.6	73.8
2003...............	79.4	93.2	93.1	93.9	78.5	86.9	76.1	73.0	72.7	71.1
2004...............	80.4	93.8	92.1	93.8	78.6	87.8	75.6	72.9	73.0	74.6
2005...............	81.0	93.2	92.1	93.8	79.4	89.0	75.5	75.5	74.7	76.4
2006...............	80.8	94.5	87.6	94.9	78.7	88.2	77.2	73.5	72.9	77.5
2007...............	80.2	92.3	89.1	90.3	78.5	86.9	76.5	74.5	72.8	77.8
2008...............	79.9	91.1	87.3	92.5	78.2	88.5	74.5	74.9	75.4	74.8
2009...............	80.2	92.6	90.7	92.9	78.7	88.7	77.4	73.6	75.3	76.1
2010...............	81.2	95.3	94.6	93.8	80.5	90.8	79.9	76.5	75.2	75.7
2011...............	82.2	92.5	88.6	93.2	81.0	92.3	78.5	76.0	75.1	80.9

NOTE: The comparability of historical labor force data has been affected at various times by methodological and other changes in the Current Population Survey (CPS). Information about historical comparability is online at **www.bls.gov/cps/documentation.htm #comp**. The women's-to-men's earnings ratios shown here are calculated from the current-dollar median usual weekly earnings of full-time wage and salary workers in table 23.

SOURCE: U.S. Bureau of Labor Statistics.

Table 14. **Women's earnings as a percent of men's, by race and Hispanic or Latino ethnicity, for full-time wage and salary workers, 1979–2011**

Year	Total, 16 years and older	White	Black or African American	Asian	Hispanic or Latino
1979	62.3	61.7	74.4	—	71.7
1980	64.2	63.4	75.8	—	73.5
1981	64.4	63.1	76.9	—	75.7
1982	65.7	64.5	78.1	—	75.5
1983	66.5	65.6	78.9	—	78.5
1984	67.6	66.8	79.5	—	77.7
1985	68.1	67.2	82.6	—	77.7
1986	69.5	67.9	82.8	—	80.6
1987	69.8	68.2	84.4	—	82.0
1988	70.2	68.4	82.8	—	84.4
1989	70.1	69.3	86.5	—	85.4
1990	71.9	71.5	85.3	—	87.4
1991	74.2	73.7	86.1	—	90.4
1992	75.8	75.3	88.2	—	89.1
1993	77.1	76.5	88.8	—	90.5
1994	76.4	74.6	86.5	—	88.9
1995	75.5	73.3	86.4	—	87.1
1996	75.0	73.8	87.9	—	88.8
1997	74.4	74.6	86.8	—	85.7
1998	76.3	76.1	85.5	—	86.4
1999	76.5	75.7	83.8	—	85.7
2000	76.9	75.8	84.1	79.9	87.8
2001	76.4	75.8	85.8	76.9	88.2
2002	77.9	77.9	90.3	74.9	88.0
2003	79.4	79.3	88.5	77.5	88.4
2004	80.4	79.8	88.8	76.4	87.3
2005	81.0	80.2	89.3	80.6	87.7
2006	80.8	80.0	87.8	79.3	87.1
2007	80.2	79.4	88.8	78.1	91.0
2008	79.9	79.3	89.4	78.0	89.6
2009	80.2	79.2	93.7	81.8	89.5
2010	81.2	80.5	93.5	82.6	90.7
2011	82.2	82.1	91.1	77.4	90.7

NOTE: The comparability of historical labor force data has been affected at various times by methodological and other changes in the Current Population Survey (CPS). Information about historical comparability is online at **www.bls.gov/cps/documentation.htm#comp**. The women's-to-men's earnings ratios shown here are calculated from the current-dollar median usual weekly earnings of full-time wage and salary workers in table 24. As of 2003, estimates for the race groups listed (White, Black or African American, and Asian) include persons who selected that race group only; persons who selected more than one race group are not included. Prior to 2003, persons who reported more than one race were included in the group they identified as the main race. Persons whose ethnicity is identified as Hispanic or Latino may be of any race. Asian data for 2000–2002 are for Asians and Pacific Islanders. As of 2003, Asians constitute a separate category. Data for Asians were not tabulated prior to 2000.

Dash indicates data not available.

SOURCE: U.S. Bureau of Labor Statistics.

Table 15. **Women's earnings as a percent of men's, by educational attainment, for full-time wage and salary workers 25 years and older, 1979–2011**

Year	Total, 25 years and older	Less than a high school diploma	High school graduates, no college	Some college or associate's degree	Bachelor's degree and higher
1979	62.1	60.3	60.1	64.1	66.7
1980	62.8	61.4	61.5	64.5	67.9
1981	62.6	61.2	61.0	65.6	66.9
1982	64.9	62.8	63.1	66.7	68.8
1983	65.8	64.8	63.4	68.2	71.2
1984	67.1	64.9	64.9	68.4	69.4
1985	66.8	64.3	65.8	67.2	70.2
1986	66.5	64.8	66.6	68.0	70.6
1987	67.3	66.0	68.1	69.8	71.4
1988	68.8	66.6	68.2	71.6	71.4
1989	70.2	66.8	67.6	73.3	71.9
1990	72.1	68.8	68.6	72.9	72.2
1991	74.0	71.6	69.8	72.6	73.6
1992	74.6	72.9	70.4	73.3	75.1
1993	74.8	73.9	71.3	73.8	75.8
1994	73.1	75.1	70.8	72.1	76.8
1995	72.8	75.5	70.2	71.6	76.2
1996	74.1	75.1	70.7	73.2	75.2
1997	75.1	75.3	70.7	73.9	75.0
1998	75.9	73.9	70.8	74.0	75.3
1999	74.4	73.4	69.8	73.4	75.7
2000	74.5	74.9	71.1	73.1	74.1
2001	75.4	75.4	72.7	71.9	73.7
2002	77.6	77.2	74.2	74.3	74.2
2003	78.5	76.7	75.5	75.7	73.6
2004	78.6	74.9	75.7	75.8	75.2
2005	79.4	74.9	75.6	76.6	75.7
2006	78.7	76.3	73.7	75.6	75.1
2007	78.5	76.7	74.3	75.2	75.0
2008	78.2	76.1	73.3	75.7	74.3
2009	78.7	76.4	75.7	75.4	73.1
2010	80.5	79.8	76.5	75.5	74.1
2011	81.0	80.9	76.9	76.8	74.9

NOTE: The comparability of historical labor force data has been affected at various times by methodological and other changes in the Current Population Survey (CPS). Information about historical comparability is online at **www.bls.gov/cps/documentation.htm#comp.** The women's-to-men's earnings ratios shown here are caculated from the current-dollar median usual weekly earnings of full-time wage and salary workers 25 years and older in table 25.

SOURCE: U.S. Bureau of Labor Statistics.

Table 16. Women's earnings as a percent of men's, by age, for wage and salary workers paid hourly rates, 1979–2011

Year	Total, 16 years and older	16 to 24 years			25 years and older					
		Total	16 to 19 years	20 to 24 years	Total	25 to 34 years	35 to 44 years	45 to 54 years	55 to 64 years	65 years and older
1979...............	64.1	81.8	95.0	75.9	58.3	63.3	55.8	54.1	56.9	87.6
1980...............	64.8	84.1	93.2	77.0	58.7	64.1	54.9	54.4	56.4	89.2
1981...............	65.1	86.1	96.7	80.0	60.3	66.7	57.5	54.1	56.2	88.1
1982...............	67.3	86.3	97.0	81.8	62.1	67.7	57.1	55.7	59.0	88.1
1983...............	69.4	87.2	96.7	84.4	62.9	70.3	57.6	56.7	58.0	87.6
1984...............	69.8	86.0	96.5	84.5	63.7	71.1	59.0	56.9	59.5	89.0
1985...............	70.0	85.7	96.3	87.2	64.7	72.4	60.3	57.8	60.4	88.8
1986...............	70.2	85.8	95.5	86.7	66.0	74.1	61.4	59.0	60.3	91.3
1987...............	72.1	85.9	93.9	86.1	67.2	74.3	62.9	61.3	62.0	91.2
1988...............	73.8	89.1	94.4	87.2	68.7	75.6	66.1	61.6	62.4	92.8
1989...............	75.4	90.7	93.4	86.9	69.8	78.0	67.0	63.4	63.8	87.1
1990...............	77.9	91.0	93.8	90.1	71.8	79.4	68.7	64.3	66.2	89.6
1991...............	78.6	91.0	97.9	91.7	73.5	80.4	70.4	65.0	68.9	92.6
1992...............	80.3	91.3	97.7	92.5	76.0	82.6	73.1	66.1	69.3	92.6
1993...............	80.4	91.7	97.1	94.2	77.3	83.6	73.1	67.3	69.0	92.1
1994...............	80.6	90.5	97.0	91.2	78.2	85.5	73.4	69.9	70.7	94.0
1995...............	80.8	90.9	96.1	89.3	76.1	83.7	72.6	70.8	71.4	94.2
1996...............	81.2	92.1	97.0	89.6	78.2	83.1	74.6	72.1	72.4	91.6
1997...............	80.8	92.2	96.6	91.2	78.8	82.7	75.7	72.3	70.5	98.1
1998...............	81.8	90.3	96.7	89.1	77.9	86.1	77.4	75.0	72.4	93.2
1999...............	83.8	92.7	96.8	89.9	79.4	83.9	76.9	72.7	76.4	95.4
2000...............	83.8	91.7	93.8	93.0	80.8	88.3	76.3	73.2	76.8	94.7
2001...............	85.2	90.5	95.8	89.7	79.2	85.8	75.0	76.1	80.2	90.4
2002...............	85.0	92.5	96.9	91.3	82.1	85.1	78.7	77.6	80.8	89.3
2003...............	84.8	93.2	97.6	91.0	83.1	87.5	79.1	79.0	78.4	90.3
2004...............	84.6	93.9	95.9	91.7	81.7	88.3	78.4	79.1	79.6	92.5
2005...............	84.8	92.6	96.0	92.4	83.2	89.2	79.6	80.2	80.2	97.8
2006...............	84.0	90.9	95.7	90.5	83.2	87.6	80.0	76.4	80.6	93.0
2007...............	84.8	89.3	95.4	90.4	81.7	87.4	81.5	79.6	79.2	92.2
2008...............	85.4	91.2	96.6	91.6	83.0	87.0	80.5	78.2	81.8	91.6
2009...............	85.5	93.1	97.1	92.0	84.7	90.6	80.7	77.0	84.5	92.6
2010...............	86.0	93.6	97.8	91.7	85.6	91.9	82.9	79.9	83.2	93.8
2011...............	86.8	94.6	97.5	92.5	86.7	92.0	83.8	81.5	82.2	91.5

NOTE: The comparability of historical labor force data has been affected at various times by methodological and other changes in the Current Population Survey (CPS). Information on historical comparability is online at **www.bls.gov/cps/documentation.htm#comp**. The women's-to-men's earnings ratios shown here are calculated from the current-dollar median hourly earnings of workers paid hourly rates in table 26.

SOURCE: U.S. Bureau of Labor Statistics.

Table 17. **Women's earnings as a percent of men's, by race and Hispanic or Latino ethnicity, for wage and salary workers paid hourly rates, 1979–2011**

Year	Total, 16 years and older	White	Black or African American	Asian	Hispanic or Latino
1979	64.1	62.5	72.6	—	71.8
1980	64.8	63.6	74.9	—	75.1
1981	65.1	63.8	72.1	—	76.4
1982	67.3	66.0	75.2	—	75.6
1983	69.4	68.0	79.2	—	76.1
1984	69.8	68.6	79.1	—	77.0
1985	70.0	67.8	82.0	—	79.4
1986	70.2	68.8	78.7	—	80.8
1987	72.1	70.9	80.1	—	80.2
1988	73.8	72.7	80.8	—	81.1
1989	75.4	74.0	83.2	—	83.0
1990	77.9	75.6	84.5	—	86.1
1991	78.6	76.6	86.5	—	86.9
1992	80.3	78.6	87.1	—	88.3
1993	80.4	78.9	89.6	—	88.6
1994	80.6	79.7	87.5	—	89.3
1995	80.8	78.4	87.3	—	90.9
1996	81.2	79.6	88.0	—	88.8
1997	80.8	80.3	87.5	—	86.3
1998	81.8	81.8	86.9	—	87.6
1999	83.8	82.3	83.2	—	86.6
2000	83.8	83.0	88.8	90.5	87.3
2001	85.2	83.8	89.9	85.1	85.6
2002	85.0	83.8	92.3	91.7	86.1
2003	84.8	84.0	91.7	89.8	88.5
2004	84.6	84.0	91.3	88.8	90.2
2005	84.8	84.2	91.1	91.3	90.1
2006	84.0	83.6	88.5	90.7	87.6
2007	84.8	83.7	90.3	89.5	88.5
2008	85.4	84.5	89.9	87.3	85.1
2009	85.5	84.8	89.7	90.4	84.6
2010	86.0	85.0	92.1	88.0	86.2
2011	86.8	85.9	93.5	89.8	86.8

NOTE: The comparability of historical labor force data has been affected at various times by methodological and other changes in the Current Population Survey (CPS). Information about historical comparability is online at **www.bls.gov/cps/documentation.htm#comp**. The women's-to-men's earnings ratios shown here are calculated from the current-dollar median hourly earnings of wage and salary workers paid hourly rates in table 27. As of 2003, estimates for the race groups listed (White, Black or African American, and Asian) include persons who selected that race group only; persons who selected more than one race group are not included. Prior to 2003, persons who reported more than one race were included in the group they identified as the main race. Persons whose ethnicity is identified as Hispanic or Latino may be of any race. Asian data for 2000–2002 are for Asians and Pacific Islanders. As of 2003, Asians constitute a separate category. Data for Asians were not tabulated prior to 2000.

Dash indicates data not available.

SOURCE: U.S. Bureau of Labor Statistics.

Table 18. **Median usual weekly earnings of full-time wage and salary workers, in constant (2011) dollars, by sex and age, 1979–2011 annual averages**

Year and sex	Total, 16 years and older	16 to 24 years			25 years and older					
		Total	16 to 19 years	20 to 24 years	Total	25 to 34 years	35 to 44 years	45 to 54 years	55 to 64 years	65 years and older
Both Sexes										
1979.................	$697	$497	$416	$538	$766	$737	$809	$798	$757	$572
1980.................	681	486	400	519	743	717	784	774	740	527
1981.................	675	475	382	506	732	703	774	760	734	527
1982.................	676	465	367	492	732	696	792	772	727	566
1983.................	672	453	352	479	736	689	794	788	742	560
1984.................	672	447	348	476	746	691	802	794	755	561
1985.................	685	446	347	478	755	695	809	797	759	592
1986.................	703	454	348	485	765	705	820	814	777	583
1987.................	708	460	352	491	763	706	824	813	767	587
1988.................	704	455	358	486	757	700	823	828	766	590
1989.................	699	454	357	483	748	690	827	827	755	585
1990.................	688	449	349	476	750	679	811	816	763	573
1991.................	686	446	343	469	752	668	802	816	755	614
1992.................	691	433	333	455	752	662	790	819	758	593
1993.................	704	433	328	456	753	669	793	831	755	603
1994.................	701	429	332	450	751	659	806	850	752	577
1995.................	702	428	339	449	748	661	806	853	754	570
1996.................	699	425	342	445	742	660	797	847	763	548
1997.................	703	427	352	448	754	672	809	848	779	549
1998.................	720	439	369	467	788	691	822	854	815	558
1999.................	741	460	379	490	799	699	825	880	815	545
2000.................	752	471	388	500	795	717	816	873	809	604
2001.................	757	476	388	501	801	732	835	881	811	620
2002.................	760	476	381	499	808	739	835	883	843	628
2003.................	758	473	380	491	809	726	840	884	866	631
2004.................	760	464	368	483	813	719	849	885	863	667
2005.................	750	457	366	474	802	703	842	862	855	656
2006.................	749	456	362	472	801	693	835	863	854	651
2007.................	754	460	366	488	800	697	834	857	871	656
2008.................	754	463	365	488	795	696	840	859	862	673
2009.................	775	463	361	486	811	711	856	878	882	717
2010.................	771	446	358	469	807	704	850	871	888	706
2011.................	756	440	352	457	797	693	837	866	881	742

See note at end of table.

Table 18. Median usual weekly earnings of full-time wage and salary workers, in constant (2011) dollars, by sex and age, 1979–2011 annual averages—cont'd

Year and sex	Total, 16 years and older	16 to 24 years			25 years and older					
		Total	16 to 19 years	20 to 24 years	Total	25 to 34 years	35 to 44 years	45 to 54 years	55 to 64 years	65 years and older
Women										
1979................	$526	$445	$382	$465	$564	$575	$566	$555	$546	$491
1980................	522	434	377	455	553	566	556	543	532	455
1981................	520	428	366	454	553	568	565	534	527	449
1982................	535	430	353	450	570	577	577	564	548	472
1983................	541	425	339	444	575	584	584	567	552	455
1984................	546	419	334	439	584	588	602	575	557	452
1985................	552	420	331	440	590	590	612	582	568	482
1986................	569	429	333	452	603	599	624	603	579	501
1987................	574	430	326	458	608	598	638	614	583	494
1988................	576	430	336	459	612	598	647	620	580	512
1989................	574	431	345	455	615	595	648	625	583	511
1990................	578	424	331	449	616	594	651	629	581	501
1991................	589	428	330	451	623	597	655	641	585	514
1992................	597	419	322	440	628	600	656	655	590	515
1993................	603	419	314	443	637	606	667	675	606	514
1994................	599	414	317	435	632	596	673	676	598	505
1995................	595	403	315	427	628	591	664	680	591	518
1996................	596	405	318	425	633	592	660	686	599	476
1997................	602	408	335	427	645	596	673	691	605	486
1998................	628	420	343	439	668	621	686	711	656	482
1999................	638	437	359	463	671	634	679	721	664	499
2000................	644	449	369	478	674	644	680	736	663	512
2001................	651	449	366	476	690	651	695	746	681	496
2002................	661	459	369	481	710	663	714	753	718	538
2003................	675	454	366	473	714	667	721	744	735	532
2004................	682	446	349	465	713	668	724	744	732	569
2005................	674	439	350	456	705	660	715	742	736	567
2006................	670	441	340	461	700	651	720	735	734	569
2007................	666	444	345	462	701	648	725	734	736	579
2008................	667	439	336	465	700	651	713	739	743	588
2009................	689	444	339	466	720	665	743	746	762	631
2010................	690	436	347	453	727	669	754	753	760	620
2011................	684	421	328	438	718	662	734	744	749	664

See note at end of table.

Table 18. Median usual weekly earnings of full-time wage and salary workers, in constant (2011) dollars, by sex and age, 1979–2011 annual averages—cont'd

| Year and sex | Total, 16 years and older | 16 to 24 years | | | 25 years and older | | | | | |
		Total	16 to 19 years	20 to 24 years	Total	25 to 34 years	35 to 44 years	45 to 54 years	55 to 64 years	65 years and older
Men										
1979	$844	$566	$448	$610	$908	$853	$971	$977	$902	$633
1980	813	540	421	582	881	816	953	953	896	595
1981	808	518	399	563	884	808	943	941	895	632
1982	814	503	380	546	879	801	944	937	893	671
1983	813	479	361	519	873	796	948	953	893	661
1984	808	476	359	515	870	788	971	969	905	676
1985	811	480	365	514	882	785	970	974	930	731
1986	820	481	364	517	906	787	977	990	947	701
1987	822	487	371	521	903	780	966	985	938	720
1988	821	479	375	510	890	770	945	1,004	931	722
1989	820	475	366	508	876	760	949	996	912	688
1990	803	471	364	497	855	750	935	987	912	673
1991	794	459	353	483	842	738	928	986	907	752
1992	786	446	342	466	841	732	912	995	909	661
1993	782	442	339	465	851	730	914	1,002	899	692
1994	784	441	342	461	865	719	926	1,008	905	662
1995	789	444	358	462	862	718	915	1,004	913	647
1996	795	438	358	458	854	712	902	996	917	680
1997	809	443	366	472	859	719	909	996	934	631
1998	824	460	387	492	880	749	933	1,008	963	664
1999	834	480	393	511	901	779	947	1,030	978	634
2000	837	490	399	516	905	781	950	1,007	960	681
2001	851	497	405	518	915	784	958	1,015	966	718
2002	849	489	390	513	915	784	949	1,009	1,003	729
2003	850	487	392	504	910	768	947	1,020	1,011	748
2004	849	476	379	496	907	761	957	1,020	1,004	763
2005	832	471	380	486	888	742	947	983	985	742
2006	829	467	388	485	890	738	933	1,001	1,007	734
2007	831	480	387	512	893	745	947	986	1,012	744
2008	834	482	386	503	896	736	956	986	985	787
2009	858	480	373	502	915	749	960	1,014	1,012	829
2010	850	457	366	483	902	737	944	985	1,010	819
2011	832	455	370	470	886	717	935	979	997	821

NOTE: The comparability of historical labor force data has been affected at various times by methodological and other changes in the Current Population Survey (CPS). Information about historical comparability is online at **www.bls.gov/cps/documentation.htm #comp**. The Consumer Price Index research series using current methods (CPI-U-RS) is used to convert current dollars to constant dollars. See the technical note.

SOURCE: U.S. Bureau of Labor Statistics.

Table 19. Median usual weekly earnings of full-time wage and salary workers, in constant (2011) dollars, by sex, race, and Hispanic or Latino ethnicity, 1979–2011 annual averages

Year and sex	Total, 16 years and older	White	Black or African American	Asian	Hispanic or Latino
Both Sexes					
1979	$697	$717	$575	—	$561
1980	681	699	551	—	543
1981	675	691	558	—	530
1982	676	694	548	—	537
1983	672	687	560	—	536
1984	672	693	555	—	534
1985	685	709	552	—	538
1986	703	726	569	—	542
1987	708	727	570	—	540
1988	704	722	574	—	530
1989	699	716	559	—	522
1990	688	708	549	—	508
1991	686	712	560	—	502
1992	691	719	560	—	504
1993	704	729	566	—	508
1994	701	727	557	—	486
1995	702	724	562	—	482
1996	699	722	552	—	484
1997	703	725	559	—	490
1998	720	751	587	—	510
1999	741	773	601	—	520
2000	752	770	619	$803	521
2001	757	775	624	812	530
2002	760	779	623	823	530
2003	758	778	623	847	538
2004	760	782	625	843	543
2005	750	774	599	868	543
2006	749	770	613	875	542
2007	754	777	617	900	546
2008	754	775	613	900	553
2009	775	794	630	922	567
2010	771	789	631	882	552
2011	756	775	613	866	549

See note at end of table.

Table 19. **Median usual weekly earnings of full-time wage and salary workers, in constant (2011) dollars, by sex, race, and Hispanic or Latino ethnicity, 1979–2011 annual averages—cont'd**

Year and sex	Total, 16 years and older	White	Black or African American	Asian	Hispanic or Latino
Women					
1979..	$526	$532	$488	—	$454
1980..	522	527	481	—	447
1981..	520	525	489	—	451
1982..	535	541	485	—	454
1983..	541	545	498	—	461
1984..	546	553	497	—	460
1985..	552	560	502	—	458
1986..	569	575	517	—	472
1987..	574	581	523	—	475
1988..	576	581	527	—	475
1989..	574	585	527	—	471
1990..	578	589	514	—	464
1991..	589	601	520	—	470
1992..	597	608	526	—	474
1993..	603	615	534	—	480
1994..	599	613	520	—	458
1995..	595	609	521	—	447
1996..	596	611	516	—	451
1997..	602	620	524	—	444
1998..	628	645	551	—	464
1999..	638	652	552	—	470
2000..	644	655	560	$714	478
2001..	651	663	577	715	493
2002..	661	684	591	708	496
2003..	675	693	600	731	501
2004..	682	695	601	730	499
2005..	674	687	575	766	494
2006..	670	680	579	780	491
2007..	666	679	578	793	513
2008..	667	683	579	787	524
2009..	689	701	610	817	534
2010..	690	706	611	798	524
2011..	684	703	595	751	518

See note at end of table.

Table 19. **Median usual weekly earnings of full-time wage and salary workers, in constant (2011) dollars, by sex, race, and Hispanic or Latino ethnicity, 1979–2011 annual averages—cont'd**

Year and sex	Total, 16 years and older	White	Black or African American	Asian	Hispanic or Latino
Men					
1979	$844	$861	$656	—	$633
1980	813	831	634	—	608
1981	808	831	637	—	596
1982	814	839	622	—	602
1983	813	830	631	—	588
1984	808	827	625	—	592
1985	811	833	608	—	590
1986	820	847	624	—	585
1987	822	852	619	—	580
1988	821	850	636	—	563
1989	820	844	609	—	552
1990	803	825	603	—	531
1991	794	815	604	—	520
1992	786	807	597	—	532
1993	782	804	601	—	531
1994	784	821	601	—	515
1995	789	830	603	—	513
1996	795	827	583	—	508
1997	809	831	603	—	518
1998	824	847	645	—	537
1999	834	861	653	—	548
2000	837	864	663	$894	544
2001	851	875	672	930	559
2002	849	878	655	945	564
2003	850	874	673	944	567
2004	849	871	677	955	571
2005	832	856	644	950	563
2006	829	849	660	984	564
2007	831	855	651	1,015	564
2008	834	862	643	1,009	584
2009	858	886	651	998	596
2010	850	877	653	966	578
2011	832	856	653	970	571

NOTE: The comparability of historical labor force data has been affected at various times by methodological and other changes in the Current Population Survey (CPS). Information about historical comparability is online at **www.bls.gov/cps/documentation.htm#comp**. As of 2003, estimates for the race groups listed (White, Black or African American, and Asian) include persons who selected that race group only; persons who selected more than one race group are not included. Prior to 2003, persons who reported more than one race were included in the group they identified as the main race. Persons whose ethnicity is identified as Hispanic or Latino may be of any race. Asian data for 2000–2002 are for Asians and Pacific Islanders. As of 2003, Asians constitute a separate category. Data for Asians were not tabulated prior to 2000. The Consumer Price Index research series using current methods (CPI-U-RS) is used to convert current dollars to constant dollars. See the technical note.

Dash indicates data not available.

SOURCE: U.S. Bureau of Labor Statistics.

Table 20. **Median usual weekly earnings of full-time wage and salary workers 25 years and older, in constant (2011) dollars, by sex and educational attainment, 1979–2011 annual averages**

Year and sex	Total, 25 years and older	Less than a high school diploma	High school graduates, no college	Some college or associate's degree	Bachelor's degree and higher
Both Sexes					
1979	$766	$607	$720	$815	$994
1980	743	577	691	790	977
1981	732	570	679	770	967
1982	732	555	676	785	980
1983	736	549	667	779	989
1984	746	542	666	788	1,002
1985	755	538	663	795	1,008
1986	765	544	673	800	1,027
1987	763	538	674	797	1,068
1988	757	527	673	786	1,069
1989	748	520	657	792	1,067
1990	750	506	644	795	1,065
1991	752	494	639	787	1,072
1992	752	488	633	760	1,093
1993	753	482	637	758	1,097
1994	751	461	632	749	1,101
1995	748	453	633	745	1,095
1996	742	452	632	739	1,081
1997	754	448	644	747	1,088
1998	788	464	660	769	1,131
1999	799	467	661	783	1,161
2000	795	473	659	778	1,163
2001	801	485	661	784	1,170
2002	808	485	669	786	1,176
2003	809	484	677	781	1,178
2004	813	477	683	787	1,174
2005	802	471	672	772	1,167
2006	801	468	664	772	1,160
2007	800	464	655	764	1,163
2008	795	473	646	754	1,165
2009	811	476	656	761	1,192
2010	807	458	646	757	1,181
2011	797	451	638	739	1,150

See note at end of table.

Table 20. **Median usual weekly earnings of full-time wage and salary workers 25 years and older, in constant (2011) dollars, by sex and educational attainment, 1979–2011 annual averages—cont'd**

Year and sex	Total, 25 years and older	Less than a high school diploma	High school graduates, no college	Some college or associate's degree	Bachelor's degree and higher
Women					
1979	$564	$439	$535	$610	$763
1980	553	426	522	600	753
1981	553	416	515	606	755
1982	570	412	528	613	774
1983	575	418	528	618	792
1984	584	412	534	629	804
1985	590	402	534	631	825
1986	603	407	542	646	853
1987	608	405	545	657	883
1988	612	404	545	658	887
1989	615	405	532	664	888
1990	616	401	526	659	893
1991	623	403	528	659	905
1992	628	402	529	639	932
1993	637	403	532	647	937
1994	632	386	527	635	952
1995	628	384	522	626	944
1996	633	382	521	631	937
1997	645	384	528	641	939
1998	668	390	545	656	974
1999	671	391	547	659	999
2000	674	397	548	659	987
2001	690	402	563	661	999
2002	710	406	573	679	1,011
2003	714	402	579	685	1,017
2004	713	398	581	687	1,024
2005	705	393	568	676	1,017
2006	700	400	558	672	1,010
2007	701	400	555	661	1,011
2008	700	395	543	656	998
2009	720	400	568	660	1,017
2010	727	400	560	658	1,018
2011	718	395	554	645	998

See note at end of table.

Table 20. **Median usual weekly earnings of full-time wage and salary workers 25 years and older, in constant (2011) dollars, by sex and educational attainment, 1979–2011 annual averages—cont'd**

Year and sex	Total, 25 years and older	Less than a high school diploma	High school graduates, no college	Some college or associate's degree	Bachelor's degree and higher
Men					
1979	$908	$728	$890	$951	$1,145
1980	881	694	849	930	1,109
1981	884	679	846	924	1,128
1982	879	655	837	919	1,125
1983	873	646	833	906	1,112
1984	870	635	823	920	1,159
1985	882	625	811	940	1,175
1986	906	628	814	949	1,209
1987	903	614	801	941	1,237
1988	890	607	799	920	1,241
1989	876	606	788	905	1,235
1990	855	583	766	905	1,237
1991	842	562	757	907	1,230
1992	841	551	752	871	1,242
1993	851	546	747	877	1,236
1994	865	514	745	881	1,240
1995	862	509	743	874	1,239
1996	854	509	736	862	1,247
1997	859	510	747	867	1,251
1998	880	528	770	886	1,293
1999	901	533	783	897	1,318
2000	905	530	772	902	1,332
2001	915	532	774	919	1,356
2002	915	526	771	914	1,363
2003	910	524	768	905	1,383
2004	907	531	768	906	1,361
2005	888	524	751	882	1,344
2006	890	523	757	888	1,345
2007	893	522	747	879	1,348
2008	896	519	741	867	1,343
2009	915	524	751	875	1,391
2010	902	502	733	872	1,373
2011	886	488	720	840	1,332

NOTE: The comparability of historical labor force data has been affected at various times by methodological and other changes in the Current Population Survey (CPS). Information about historical comparability is online at **www.bls.gov/cps/documentation.htm#comp**. The Consumer Price Index research series using current methods (CPI-U-RS) is used to convert current dollars to constant dollars. See the technical note.

SOURCE: U.S. Bureau of Labor Statistics.

Table 21. **Median hourly earnings of wage and salary workers paid hourly rates, in constant (2011) dollars, by sex and age, 1979–2011 annual averages**

Year and sex	Total, 16 years and older	16 to 24 years			25 years and older					
		Total	16 to 19 years	20 to 24 years	Total	25 to 34 years	35 to 44 years	45 to 54 years	55 to 64 years	65 years and older
Both Sexes										
1979.............	$12.83	$10.09	$8.96	$11.62	$14.77	$15.03	$15.29	$14.91	$14.36	$9.34
1980.............	12.52	9.64	8.36	11.14	14.42	14.70	14.96	14.68	14.00	9.25
1981.............	12.23	9.43	8.50	10.95	14.23	14.47	14.73	14.28	13.80	9.31
1982.............	12.08	9.06	8.05	10.43	14.05	14.21	14.79	14.36	13.67	9.22
1983.............	12.00	8.76	7.75	10.06	14.06	13.95	14.83	14.44	13.76	9.44
1984.............	12.02	8.62	7.53	9.94	14.10	13.96	14.78	14.60	13.65	9.55
1985.............	12.01	8.49	7.31	9.84	14.04	13.78	14.92	14.68	13.76	9.44
1986.............	12.13	8.63	7.26	9.90	14.15	13.72	15.24	15.13	14.03	9.73
1987.............	12.25	8.69	7.22	9.87	14.13	13.62	15.04	14.89	14.05	9.62
1988.............	12.30	8.76	7.37	9.84	14.15	13.58	14.94	14.92	13.67	9.56
1989.............	12.24	8.67	7.39	9.89	13.91	13.38	14.99	14.75	13.70	9.49
1990.............	12.07	8.61	7.50	9.87	13.62	13.19	14.72	14.67	13.39	9.60
1991.............	12.08	8.47	7.55	9.66	13.66	12.95	14.77	14.67	13.19	9.57
1992.............	12.12	8.43	7.43	9.47	13.70	12.83	14.73	14.95	13.31	9.64
1993.............	12.07	8.45	7.36	9.43	13.73	12.68	14.74	15.12	13.65	9.80
1994.............	12.03	8.44	7.37	9.34	13.69	12.58	14.89	15.05	13.54	9.59
1995.............	11.98	8.50	7.39	9.41	13.72	12.77	14.69	14.85	13.49	9.75
1996.............	11.98	8.47	7.38	9.54	13.72	12.58	14.47	14.61	13.40	9.66
1997.............	12.22	8.59	7.70	9.65	13.78	12.63	14.47	14.80	13.59	9.62
1998.............	12.53	9.06	8.10	9.97	13.95	13.29	14.96	15.10	13.88	10.19
1999.............	12.86	9.27	8.21	10.45	14.13	13.47	14.87	15.29	14.01	10.39
2000.............	12.94	9.45	8.37	10.54	14.20	13.29	14.82	15.43	14.13	10.51
2001.............	12.95	9.77	8.59	10.65	14.49	13.56	15.21	15.46	14.45	10.84
2002.............	13.09	9.76	8.64	10.59	14.79	13.73	15.23	15.58	14.81	11.34
2003.............	13.26	9.66	8.47	10.59	14.73	13.75	15.23	15.86	14.90	11.23
2004.............	13.10	9.50	8.33	10.45	14.56	13.54	15.35	15.75	14.98	11.45
2005.............	12.89	9.30	8.12	10.26	14.38	13.55	15.10	15.53	14.92	11.44
2006.............	13.13	9.20	8.07	10.22	14.44	13.34	15.06	15.66	14.88	11.33
2007.............	12.96	9.38	8.21	10.48	14.27	13.07	15.11	15.61	14.87	11.25
2008.............	12.78	9.27	8.19	10.20	14.43	13.06	15.03	15.54	14.84	11.38
2009.............	13.04	9.33	8.30	10.24	14.58	13.21	15.29	15.57	15.41	12.04
2010.............	12.90	9.18	8.26	9.83	14.43	12.93	15.08	15.46	15.37	11.92
2011.............	12.71	8.97	8.06	9.61	14.12	12.71	14.83	15.00	15.07	12.19

See note at end of table.

Table 21. Median hourly earnings of wage and salary workers paid hourly rates, in constant (2011) dollars, by sex and age, 1979–2011 annual averages—cont'd

Year and sex	Total, 16 years and older	16 to 24 years			25 years and older					
		Total	16 to 19 years	20 to 24 years	Total	25 to 34 years	35 to 44 years	45 to 54 years	55 to 64 years	65 years and older
Women										
1979................	$10.46	$9.22	$8.76	$10.17	$11.27	$11.68	$11.47	$11.10	$10.84	$9.02
1980................	10.26	8.96	8.16	9.84	11.01	11.53	11.14	10.99	10.60	8.78
1981................	10.17	8.81	8.36	9.71	11.14	11.62	11.33	10.90	10.52	8.81
1982................	10.31	8.46	7.94	9.37	11.23	11.61	11.36	11.07	10.74	8.79
1983................	10.30	8.20	7.62	9.14	11.22	11.67	11.39	11.14	10.88	8.93
1984................	10.25	8.10	7.40	8.99	11.30	11.55	11.57	11.36	10.87	9.01
1985................	10.22	7.99	7.19	9.08	11.41	11.53	11.77	11.47	10.88	8.82
1986................	10.43	8.04	7.14	9.22	11.64	11.64	12.00	11.72	11.25	9.26
1987................	10.61	7.99	7.03	9.26	11.67	11.63	12.03	11.89	11.42	9.19
1988................	10.68	8.19	7.15	9.23	11.77	11.63	12.36	12.05	11.12	9.36
1989................	10.70	8.21	7.18	9.16	11.87	11.70	12.43	12.08	11.17	9.00
1990................	10.75	8.26	7.26	9.30	11.80	11.70	12.30	11.95	11.24	9.10
1991................	10.87	8.18	7.47	9.19	11.82	11.58	12.45	12.25	11.19	9.28
1992................	10.93	8.10	7.36	9.06	12.01	11.70	12.54	12.46	11.30	9.37
1993................	10.92	8.08	7.25	9.14	12.07	11.67	12.52	12.55	11.60	9.48
1994................	10.89	7.99	7.25	8.98	12.09	11.68	12.67	12.70	11.74	9.37
1995................	10.94	8.05	7.24	8.93	11.98	11.61	12.65	12.79	11.63	9.46
1996................	11.03	8.10	7.26	8.93	12.03	11.50	12.68	12.75	11.51	9.20
1997................	11.09	8.31	7.57	9.15	12.22	11.45	12.77	12.93	11.61	9.54
1998................	11.34	8.60	7.96	9.55	12.58	12.12	13.31	13.47	12.19	9.93
1999................	11.66	8.91	8.07	9.74	12.86	12.28	13.27	13.43	12.59	10.12
2000................	11.83	9.14	8.13	10.18	12.91	12.65	13.09	13.29	12.85	10.27
2001................	12.25	9.21	8.40	10.17	12.96	12.63	13.27	13.79	13.20	10.34
2002................	12.36	9.31	8.50	10.14	13.39	12.65	13.73	13.98	13.51	10.91
2003................	12.32	9.28	8.37	10.01	13.46	12.85	13.66	14.41	13.51	10.81
2004................	12.11	9.18	8.17	9.90	13.37	12.64	13.63	14.23	13.77	10.90
2005................	11.88	8.99	7.97	9.79	13.34	12.51	13.64	13.97	13.66	11.31
2006................	11.89	8.92	7.94	9.84	13.25	12.35	13.45	13.68	13.53	11.13
2007................	11.91	8.84	8.04	9.76	13.07	12.16	13.41	13.94	13.26	11.01
2008................	12.01	8.81	8.06	9.57	13.04	12.25	13.47	13.75	13.58	11.00
2009................	12.33	8.99	8.20	9.63	13.38	12.54	13.63	13.72	14.25	11.65
2010................	12.21	8.90	8.16	9.37	13.29	12.43	13.54	13.93	14.12	11.54
2011................	11.98	8.73	7.96	9.16	13.10	12.12	13.44	13.76	14.03	11.76

See note at end of table.

Table 21. Median hourly earnings of wage and salary workers paid hourly rates, in constant (2011) dollars, by sex and age, 1979–2011 annual averages—cont'd

Year and sex	Total, 16 years and older	16 to 24 years			25 years and older					
		Total	16 to 19 years	20 to 24 years	Total	25 to 34 years	35 to 44 years	45 to 54 years	55 to 64 years	65 years and older
Men										
1979	$16.33	$11.27	$9.22	$13.41	$19.34	$18.44	$20.58	$20.52	$19.05	$10.29
1980	15.84	10.65	8.75	12.78	18.75	18.00	20.29	20.21	18.81	9.84
1981	15.61	10.24	8.65	12.14	18.48	17.41	19.71	20.17	18.72	10.00
1982	15.32	9.80	8.19	11.45	18.08	17.16	19.89	19.87	18.21	9.98
1983	14.85	9.40	7.88	10.84	17.83	16.61	19.79	19.66	18.76	10.19
1984	14.68	9.42	7.67	10.64	17.73	16.25	19.61	19.98	18.27	10.12
1985	14.60	9.32	7.47	10.42	17.63	15.94	19.52	19.86	18.01	9.94
1986	14.85	9.37	7.48	10.63	17.65	15.71	19.55	19.86	18.67	10.14
1987	14.72	9.30	7.48	10.76	17.35	15.64	19.13	19.39	18.41	10.08
1988	14.46	9.20	7.57	10.59	17.15	15.37	18.68	19.54	17.81	10.09
1989	14.19	9.05	7.69	10.54	17.01	14.99	18.55	19.05	17.51	10.33
1990	13.81	9.08	7.75	10.32	16.43	14.74	17.91	18.58	16.98	10.15
1991	13.83	8.99	7.63	10.03	16.07	14.40	17.68	18.86	16.23	10.02
1992	13.61	8.87	7.54	9.80	15.79	14.16	17.16	18.87	16.31	10.13
1993	13.59	8.82	7.47	9.71	15.61	13.96	17.12	18.63	16.81	10.29
1994	13.51	8.83	7.48	9.85	15.45	13.66	17.27	18.17	16.61	9.97
1995	13.53	8.86	7.54	10.00	15.73	13.87	17.43	18.06	16.29	10.04
1996	13.58	8.80	7.49	9.97	15.38	13.84	16.99	17.69	15.91	10.04
1997	13.73	9.01	7.84	10.03	15.50	13.85	16.86	17.88	16.47	9.72
1998	13.86	9.52	8.24	10.72	16.14	14.08	17.19	17.96	16.83	10.66
1999	13.91	9.61	8.34	10.84	16.19	14.63	17.25	18.46	16.48	10.61
2000	14.11	9.96	8.67	10.95	15.98	14.32	17.15	18.15	16.72	10.85
2001	14.38	10.18	8.77	11.33	16.37	14.71	17.69	18.11	16.45	11.44
2002	14.55	10.06	8.78	11.10	16.31	14.86	17.45	18.00	16.73	12.23
2003	14.54	9.95	8.58	11.00	16.20	14.68	17.27	18.25	17.22	11.97
2004	14.31	9.77	8.51	10.80	16.36	14.32	17.38	17.99	17.31	11.79
2005	14.01	9.70	8.31	10.60	16.03	14.02	17.14	17.43	17.04	11.57
2006	14.15	9.81	8.29	10.88	15.93	14.10	16.81	17.90	16.79	11.96
2007	14.05	9.90	8.43	10.80	16.00	13.92	16.45	17.52	16.76	11.94
2008	14.06	9.66	8.34	10.45	15.71	14.08	16.74	17.58	16.61	12.02
2009	14.42	9.66	8.44	10.47	15.80	13.84	16.88	17.81	16.87	12.58
2010	14.20	9.50	8.35	10.22	15.52	13.52	16.34	17.43	16.98	12.30
2011	13.80	9.23	8.16	9.90	15.11	13.18	16.03	16.88	17.07	12.85

NOTE: The comparability of historical labor force data has been affected at various times by methodological and other changes in the Current Population Survey (CPS). Information about historical comparability is online at **www.bls.gov/cps/documentation.htm #comp**. The Consumer Price Index research series using current methods (CPI-U-RS) is used to convert current dollars to constant dollars. See the technical note.

SOURCE: U.S. Bureau of Labor Statistics.

Table 22. **Median hourly earnings of wage and salary workers paid hourly rates, in constant (2011) dollars, by sex, race, and Hispanic or Latino ethnicity, 1979–2011 annual averages**

Year and sex	Total, 16 years and older	White	Black or African American	Asian	Hispanic or Latino
Both Sexes					
1979..	$12.83	$13.03	$11.88	—	$11.79
1980..	12.52	12.68	11.53	—	11.53
1981..	12.23	12.30	11.64	—	11.43
1982..	12.08	12.24	11.32	—	11.21
1983..	12.00	12.15	11.05	—	10.92
1984..	12.02	12.16	11.05	—	10.87
1985..	12.01	12.15	10.96	—	10.90
1986..	12.13	12.29	11.35	—	11.06
1987..	12.25	12.42	11.34	—	11.02
1988..	12.30	12.45	11.24	—	10.88
1989..	12.24	12.40	11.26	—	10.63
1990..	12.07	12.24	11.37	—	10.48
1991..	12.08	12.25	11.27	—	10.40
1992..	12.12	12.28	11.08	—	10.44
1993..	12.07	12.22	11.01	—	10.48
1994..	12.03	12.18	10.95	—	10.41
1995..	11.98	12.20	11.23	—	10.26
1996..	11.98	12.23	11.07	—	10.23
1997..	12.22	12.40	11.19	—	10.32
1998..	12.53	12.70	11.56	—	10.91
1999..	12.86	13.14	11.94	—	10.89
2000..	12.94	13.00	12.19	$13.15	11.15
2001..	12.95	13.04	12.43	13.66	11.51
2002..	13.09	13.39	12.41	12.95	11.53
2003..	13.26	13.41	12.41	13.59	11.93
2004..	13.10	13.25	12.13	13.21	11.68
2005..	12.89	13.23	11.72	13.84	11.46
2006..	13.13	13.24	11.90	13.98	11.29
2007..	12.96	13.10	11.81	13.25	11.11
2008..	12.78	13.10	11.70	13.59	11.46
2009..	13.04	13.27	12.20	13.79	11.57
2010..	12.90	13.15	12.15	13.64	11.23
2011..	12.71	12.91	11.79	13.35	11.05

See note at end of table.

Table 22. **Median hourly earnings of wage and salary workers paid hourly rates, in constant (2011) dollars, by sex, race, and Hispanic or Latino ethnicity, 1979–2011 annual averages—cont'd**

Year and sex	Total, 16 years and older	White	Black or African American	Asian	Hispanic or Latino
Women					
1979..	$10.46	$10.46	$10.26	—	$9.94
1980..	10.26	10.29	10.08	—	9.82
1981..	10.17	10.17	9.95	—	9.74
1982..	10.31	10.31	10.04	—	9.69
1983..	10.30	10.32	10.13	—	9.48
1984..	10.25	10.27	10.04	—	9.59
1985..	10.22	10.24	10.04	—	9.60
1986..	10.43	10.47	10.12	—	9.78
1987..	10.61	10.64	10.23	—	9.68
1988..	10.68	10.71	10.26	—	9.65
1989..	10.70	10.74	10.30	—	9.68
1990..	10.75	10.78	10.40	—	9.68
1991..	10.87	10.89	10.55	—	9.63
1992..	10.93	10.97	10.42	—	9.69
1993..	10.92	10.98	10.54	—	9.68
1994..	10.89	11.02	10.41	—	9.61
1995..	10.94	11.06	10.44	—	9.68
1996..	11.03	11.11	10.27	—	9.66
1997..	11.09	11.17	10.60	—	9.53
1998..	11.34	11.47	10.88	—	9.94
1999..	11.66	11.78	10.97	—	10.07
2000..	11.83	11.87	11.57	$12.75	10.30
2001..	12.25	12.36	11.63	12.80	10.52
2002..	12.36	12.43	11.81	12.63	10.68
2003..	12.32	12.36	12.11	13.06	10.86
2004..	12.11	12.15	11.82	12.58	10.76
2005..	11.88	12.10	11.44	13.41	10.58
2006..	11.89	12.02	11.28	13.34	10.60
2007..	11.91	12.00	11.33	12.83	10.63
2008..	12.01	12.23	11.26	12.80	10.52
2009..	12.33	12.40	11.54	13.28	10.58
2010..	12.21	12.26	11.56	12.81	10.43
2011..	11.98	12.05	11.28	12.80	10.25

See note at end of table.

Table 22. **Median hourly earnings of wage and salary workers paid hourly rates, in constant (2011) dollars, by sex, race, and Hispanic or Latino ethnicity, 1979–2011 annual averages—cont'd**

Year and sex	Total, 16 years and older	White	Black or African American	Asian	Hispanic or Latino
Men					
1979	$16.33	$16.73	$14.13	—	$13.84
1980	15.84	16.18	13.45	—	13.06
1981	15.61	15.94	13.80	—	12.76
1982	15.32	15.62	13.36	—	12.82
1983	14.85	15.17	12.79	—	12.47
1984	14.68	14.97	12.70	—	12.45
1985	14.60	15.10	12.25	—	12.09
1986	14.85	15.23	12.86	—	12.11
1987	14.72	15.02	12.77	—	12.06
1988	14.46	14.73	12.69	—	11.90
1989	14.19	14.50	12.38	—	11.66
1990	13.81	14.27	12.30	—	11.25
1991	13.83	14.20	12.19	—	11.08
1992	13.61	13.96	11.96	—	10.97
1993	13.59	13.91	11.76	—	10.92
1994	13.51	13.83	11.89	—	10.77
1995	13.53	14.11	11.96	—	10.65
1996	13.58	13.97	11.67	—	10.87
1997	13.73	13.91	12.11	—	11.03
1998	13.86	14.02	12.52	—	11.35
1999	13.91	14.32	13.18	—	11.62
2000	14.11	14.30	13.03	$14.09	11.80
2001	14.38	14.75	12.94	15.04	12.29
2002	14.55	14.83	12.80	13.78	12.40
2003	14.54	14.71	13.22	14.54	12.26
2004	14.31	14.48	12.95	14.17	11.93
2005	14.01	14.37	12.56	14.69	11.74
2006	14.15	14.38	12.75	14.71	12.10
2007	14.05	14.34	12.55	14.34	12.01
2008	14.06	14.47	12.53	14.66	12.36
2009	14.42	14.62	12.86	14.69	12.49
2010	14.20	14.42	12.55	14.56	12.11
2011	13.80	14.02	12.06	14.25	11.81

NOTE: The comparability of historical labor force data has been affected at various times by methodological and other changes in the Current Population Survey (CPS). Information about historical comparability is online at **www.bls.gov/cps/documentation.htm#comp**. As of 2003, estimates for the race groups listed (White, Black or African American, and Asian) include persons who selected that race group only; persons who selected more than one race group are not included. Prior to 2003, persons who reported more than one race were included in the group they identified as the main race. Persons whose ethnicity is identified as Hispanic or Latino may be of any race. Asian data for 2000–2002 are for Asians and Pacific Islanders. As of 2003, Asians constitute a separate category. Data for Asians were not tabulated prior to 2000. The Consumer Price Index research series using current methods (CPI-U-RS) is used to convert current dollars to constant dollars. See the technical note.

Dash indicates data not available.

SOURCE: U.S. Bureau of Labor Statistics.

Table 23. Median usual weekly earnings of full-time wage and salary workers, in current dollars, by sex and age, 1979–2011 annual averages

Year and sex	Total, 16 years and older	16 to 24 years			25 years and older					
		Total	16 to 19 years	20 to 24 years	Total	25 to 34 years	35 to 44 years	45 to 54 years	55 to 64 years	65 years and older
Both Sexes										
1979..............	$241	$172	$144	$186	$265	$255	$280	$276	$262	$198
1980..............	262	187	154	200	286	276	302	298	285	203
1981..............	284	200	161	213	308	296	326	320	309	222
1982..............	302	208	164	220	327	311	354	345	325	253
1983..............	313	211	164	223	343	321	370	367	346	261
1984..............	326	217	169	231	362	335	389	385	366	272
1985..............	344	224	174	240	379	349	406	400	381	297
1986..............	359	232	178	248	391	360	419	416	397	298
1987..............	374	243	186	259	403	373	435	429	405	310
1988..............	385	249	196	266	414	383	450	453	419	323
1989..............	399	259	204	276	427	394	472	472	431	334
1990..............	412	269	209	285	449	407	486	489	457	343
1991..............	426	277	213	291	467	415	498	507	469	381
1992..............	440	276	212	290	479	422	503	522	483	378
1993..............	459	282	214	297	491	436	517	542	492	393
1994..............	467	286	221	300	500	439	537	566	501	384
1995..............	479	292	231	306	510	451	550	582	514	389
1996..............	490	298	240	312	520	463	559	594	535	384
1997..............	503	306	252	321	540	481	579	607	558	393
1998..............	523	319	268	339	572	502	597	620	592	405
1999..............	549	341	281	363	592	518	611	652	604	404
2000..............	576	361	297	383	609	549	625	669	620	463
2001..............	596	375	305	394	630	576	657	693	638	488
2002..............	608	381	305	399	646	591	668	706	674	502
2003..............	620	387	311	402	662	594	687	723	708	516
2004..............	638	390	309	406	683	604	713	743	725	560
2005..............	651	397	318	411	696	610	731	748	742	569
2006..............	671	409	324	423	718	621	748	773	765	583
2007..............	695	424	337	450	738	643	769	790	803	605
2008..............	722	443	349	467	761	666	804	822	825	644
2009..............	739	442	344	464	774	678	817	838	841	684
2010..............	747	432	347	454	782	682	824	844	860	684
2011..............	756	440	352	457	797	693	837	866	881	742

See note at end of table.

75

Table 23. **Median usual weekly earnings of full-time wage and salary workers, in current dollars, by sex and age, 1979–2011 annual averages—cont'd**

Year and sex	Total, 16 years and older	16 to 24 years			25 years and older					
		Total	16 to 19 years	20 to 24 years	Total	25 to 34 years	35 to 44 years	45 to 54 years	55 to 64 years	65 years and older
Women										
1979.................	$182	$154	$132	$161	$195	$199	$196	$192	$189	$170
1980.................	201	167	145	175	213	218	214	209	205	175
1981.................	219	180	154	191	233	239	238	225	222	189
1982.................	239	192	158	201	255	258	258	252	245	211
1983.................	252	198	158	207	268	272	272	264	257	212
1984.................	265	203	162	213	283	285	292	279	270	219
1985.................	277	211	166	221	296	296	307	292	285	242
1986.................	291	219	170	231	308	306	319	308	296	256
1987.................	303	227	172	242	321	316	337	324	308	261
1988.................	315	235	184	251	335	327	354	339	317	280
1989.................	328	246	197	260	351	340	370	357	333	292
1990.................	346	254	198	269	369	356	390	377	348	300
1991.................	366	266	205	280	387	371	407	398	363	319
1992.................	380	267	205	280	400	382	418	417	376	328
1993.................	393	273	205	289	415	395	435	440	395	335
1994.................	399	276	211	290	421	397	448	450	398	336
1995.................	406	275	215	291	428	403	453	464	403	353
1996.................	418	284	223	298	444	415	463	481	420	334
1997.................	431	292	240	306	462	427	482	495	433	348
1998.................	456	305	249	319	485	451	498	516	476	350
1999.................	473	324	266	343	497	470	503	534	492	370
2000.................	493	344	283	366	516	493	521	564	508	392
2001.................	512	353	288	375	543	512	547	587	536	390
2002.................	529	367	295	385	568	530	571	602	574	430
2003.................	552	371	299	387	584	546	590	609	601	435
2004.................	573	375	293	391	599	561	608	625	615	478
2005.................	585	381	304	396	612	573	621	644	639	492
2006.................	600	395	305	413	627	583	645	659	658	510
2007.................	614	409	318	426	646	597	668	677	679	534
2008.................	638	420	322	445	670	623	682	707	711	563
2009.................	657	424	323	445	687	634	709	712	727	602
2010.................	669	422	336	439	704	648	731	730	736	601
2011.................	684	421	328	438	718	662	734	744	749	664

See note at end of table.

Table 23. Median usual weekly earnings of full-time wage and salary workers, in current dollars, by sex and age, 1979–2011 annual averages—cont'd

Year and sex	Total, 16 years and older	16 to 24 years			25 years and older					
		Total	16 to 19 years	20 to 24 years	Total	25 to 34 years	35 to 44 years	45 to 54 years	55 to 64 years	65 years and older
Men										
1979..............	$292	$196	$155	$211	$314	$295	$336	$338	$312	$219
1980..............	313	208	162	224	339	314	367	367	345	229
1981..............	340	218	168	237	372	340	397	396	377	266
1982..............	364	225	170	244	393	358	422	419	399	300
1983..............	379	223	168	242	407	371	442	444	416	308
1984..............	392	231	174	250	422	382	471	470	439	328
1985..............	407	241	183	258	443	394	487	489	467	367
1986..............	419	246	186	264	463	402	499	506	484	358
1987..............	434	257	196	275	477	412	510	520	495	380
1988..............	449	262	205	279	487	421	517	549	509	395
1989..............	468	271	209	290	500	434	542	569	521	393
1990..............	481	282	218	298	512	449	560	591	546	403
1991..............	493	285	219	300	523	458	576	612	563	467
1992..............	501	284	218	297	536	466	581	634	579	421
1993..............	510	288	221	303	555	476	596	653	586	451
1994..............	522	294	228	307	576	479	617	671	603	441
1995..............	538	303	244	315	588	490	624	685	623	441
1996..............	557	307	251	321	599	499	632	698	643	477
1997..............	579	317	262	338	615	515	651	713	669	452
1998..............	598	334	281	357	639	544	677	732	699	482
1999..............	618	356	291	379	668	577	702	763	725	470
2000..............	641	375	306	395	693	598	728	771	735	522
2001..............	670	391	319	408	720	617	754	799	760	565
2002..............	679	391	312	410	732	627	759	807	802	583
2003..............	695	398	321	412	744	628	775	834	827	612
2004..............	713	400	318	417	762	639	804	857	843	641
2005..............	722	409	330	422	771	644	822	853	855	644
2006..............	743	418	348	435	797	661	836	897	902	658
2007..............	766	443	357	472	823	687	873	909	933	686
2008..............	798	461	369	481	857	704	915	944	943	753
2009..............	819	458	356	479	873	715	916	967	965	791
2010..............	824	443	355	468	874	714	915	954	979	794
2011..............	832	455	370	470	886	717	935	979	997	821

NOTE: The comparability of historical labor force data has been affected at various times by methodological and other changes in the Current Population Survey (CPS). Information about historical comparability is online at **www.bls.gov/cps/documentation.htm #comp**.

SOURCE: U.S. Bureau of Labor Statistics.

Table 24. **Median usual weekly earnings of full-time wage and salary workers, in current dollars, by sex, race, and Hispanic or Latino ethnicity, 1979–2011 annual averages**

Year and sex	Total, 16 years and older	White	Black or African American	Asian	Hispanic or Latino
Both Sexes					
1979	$241	$248	$199	—	$194
1980	262	269	212	—	209
1981	284	291	235	—	223
1982	302	310	245	—	240
1983	313	320	261	—	250
1984	326	336	269	—	259
1985	344	356	277	—	270
1986	359	371	291	—	277
1987	374	384	301	—	285
1988	385	395	314	—	290
1989	399	409	319	—	298
1990	412	424	329	—	304
1991	426	442	348	—	312
1992	440	458	357	—	321
1993	459	475	369	—	331
1994	467	484	371	—	324
1995	479	494	383	—	329
1996	490	506	387	—	339
1997	503	519	400	—	351
1998	523	545	426	—	370
1999	549	573	445	—	385
2000	576	590	474	$615	399
2001	596	610	491	639	417
2002	608	623	498	658	424
2003	620	636	514	693	440
2004	638	657	525	708	456
2005	651	672	520	753	471
2006	671	690	554	784	486
2007	695	716	569	830	503
2008	722	742	589	861	529
2009	739	757	601	880	541
2010	747	765	611	855	535
2011	756	775	615	866	549

See note at end of table.

Table 24. **Median usual weekly earnings of full-time wage and salary workers, in current dollars, by sex, race, and Hispanic or Latino ethnicity, 1979–2011 annual averages—cont'd**

Year and sex	Total, 16 years and older	White	Black or African American	Asian	Hispanic or Latino
Women					
1979	$182	$184	$169	—	$157
1980	201	203	185	—	172
1981	219	221	206	—	190
1982	239	242	217	—	203
1983	252	254	232	—	215
1984	265	268	241	—	223
1985	277	281	252	—	230
1986	291	294	264	—	241
1987	303	307	276	—	251
1988	315	318	288	—	260
1989	328	334	301	—	269
1990	346	353	308	—	278
1991	366	373	323	—	292
1992	380	387	335	—	302
1993	393	401	348	—	313
1994	399	408	346	—	305
1995	406	415	355	—	305
1996	418	428	362	—	316
1997	431	444	375	—	318
1998	456	468	400	—	337
1999	473	483	409	—	348
2000	493	502	429	$547	366
2001	512	522	454	563	388
2002	529	547	473	566	397
2003	552	567	491	598	410
2004	573	584	505	613	419
2005	585	596	499	665	429
2006	600	609	519	699	440
2007	614	626	533	731	473
2008	638	654	554	753	501
2009	657	669	582	779	509
2010	669	684	592	773	508
2011	684	703	595	751	518

See note at end of table.

Table 24. **Median usual weekly earnings of full-time wage and salary workers, in current dollars, by sex, race, and Hispanic or Latino ethnicity, 1979–2011 annual averages—cont'd**

Year and sex	Total, 16 years and older	White	Black or African American	Asian	Hispanic or Latino
Men					
1979..	$292	$298	$227	—	$219
1980..	313	320	244	—	234
1981..	340	350	268	—	251
1982..	364	375	278	—	269
1983..	379	387	294	—	274
1984..	392	401	303	—	287
1985..	407	418	305	—	296
1986..	419	433	319	—	299
1987..	434	450	327	—	306
1988..	449	465	348	—	308
1989..	468	482	348	—	315
1990..	481	494	361	—	318
1991..	493	506	375	—	323
1992..	501	514	380	—	339
1993..	510	524	392	—	346
1994..	522	547	400	—	343
1995..	538	566	411	—	350
1996..	557	580	412	—	356
1997..	579	595	432	—	371
1998..	598	615	468	—	390
1999..	618	638	488	—	406
2000..	641	662	510	$685	417
2001..	670	689	529	732	440
2002..	679	702	524	756	451
2003..	695	715	555	772	464
2004..	713	732	569	802	480
2005..	722	743	559	825	489
2006..	743	761	591	882	505
2007..	766	788	600	936	520
2008..	798	825	620	966	559
2009..	819	845	621	952	569
2010..	824	850	633	936	560
2011..	832	856	653	970	571

NOTE: The comparability of historical labor force data has been affected at various times by methodological and other changes in the Current Population Survey (CPS). Information about historical comparability is online at **www.bls.gov/cps/documentation.htm#comp**. As of 2003, estimates for the race groups listed (White, Black or African American, and Asian) include persons who selected that race group only; persons who selected more than one race group are not included. Prior to 2003, persons who reported more than one race were included in the group they identified as the main race. Persons whose ethnicity is identified as Hispanic or Latino may be of any race. Asian data for 2000–2002 are for Asians and Pacific Islanders. As of 2003, Asians constitute a separate category. Data for Asians were not tabulated prior to 2000.

Dash indicates data not available.

SOURCE: U.S. Bureau of Labor Statistics.

Table 25. **Median usual weekly earnings of full-time wage and salary workers 25 years and older, in current dollars, by sex and educational attainment, 1979–2011 annual averages**

Year and sex	Total, 25 years and older	Less than a high school diploma	High school graduates, no college	Some college or associate's degree	Bachelor's degree and higher
Both Sexes					
1979	$265	$210	$249	$282	$344
1980	286	222	266	304	376
1981	308	240	286	324	407
1982	327	248	302	351	438
1983	343	256	3·1	363	461
1984	362	263	323	382	486
1985	379	270	333	399	506
1986	391	278	344	409	525
1987	403	284	356	421	564
1988	414	288	368	430	585
1989	427	297	3¯5	452	609
1990	449	303	386	476	638
1991	467	307	397	489	666
1992	479	311	403	484	696
1993	491	314	415	494	715
1994	500	307	421	499	733
1995	510	309	432	508	747
1996	520	317	443	518	758
1997	540	321	461	535	779
1998	572	337	4¯9	558	821
1999	592	346	490	580	860
2000	609	362	505	596	891
2001	630	382	520	617	921
2002	646	388	535	629	941
2003	662	396	5·4	639	964
2004	683	401	574	661	986
2005	696	409	533	670	1,013
2006	718	419	5·5	692	1,039
2007	738	428	6·4	704	1,072
2008	761	453	618	722	1,115
2009	774	454	626	726	1,137
2010	782	444	626	734	1,144
2011	797	451	638	739	1,150

See note at end of table.

Table 25. Median usual weekly earnings of full-time wage and salary workers 25 years and older, in current dollars, by sex and educational attainment, 1979–2011 annual averages—cont'd

Year and sex	Total, 25 years and older	Less than a high school diploma	High school graduates, no college	Some college or associate's degree	Bachelor's degree and higher
Women					
1979..	$195	$152	$185	$211	$264
1980..	213	164	201	231	290
1981..	233	175	217	255	318
1982..	255	184	236	274	346
1983..	268	195	246	288	369
1984..	283	200	259	305	390
1985..	296	202	268	317	414
1986..	308	208	277	330	436
1987..	321	214	288	347	466
1988..	335	221	298	360	485
1989..	351	231	304	379	507
1990..	369	240	315	395	535
1991..	387	250	328	409	562
1992..	400	256	337	407	594
1993..	415	263	347	422	611
1994..	421	257	351	423	634
1995..	428	262	356	427	644
1996..	444	268	365	442	657
1997..	462	275	378	459	672
1998..	485	283	396	476	707
1999..	497	290	405	488	740
2000..	516	304	420	505	756
2001..	543	316	443	520	786
2002..	568	325	458	543	809
2003..	584	329	474	560	832
2004..	599	334	488	577	860
2005..	612	341	493	587	883
2006..	627	358	500	602	905
2007..	646	369	512	609	932
2008..	670	378	520	628	955
2009..	687	382	542	630	970
2010..	704	388	543	638	986
2011..	718	395	554	645	998

See note at end of table.

Table 25. Median usual weekly earnings of full-time wage and salary workers 25 years and older, in current dollars, by sex and educational attainment, 1979–2011 annual averages—cont'd

Year and sex	Total, 25 years and older	Less than a high school diploma	High school graduates, no college	Some college or associate's degree	Bachelor's degree and higher
Men					
1979	$314	$252	$308	$329	$396
1980	339	267	327	358	427
1981	372	286	356	389	475
1982	393	293	374	411	503
1983	407	301	388	422	518
1984	422	308	399	446	562
1985	443	314	407	472	590
1986	463	321	416	485	618
1987	477	324	423	497	653
1988	487	332	437	503	679
1989	500	346	450	517	705
1990	512	349	459	542	741
1991	523	349	470	563	764
1992	536	351	479	555	791
1993	555	356	487	572	806
1994	576	342	496	587	826
1995	588	347	507	596	845
1996	599	357	516	604	874
1997	615	365	535	621	896
1998	639	383	559	643	939
1999	668	395	580	665	977
2000	693	406	591	691	1,020
2001	720	419	609	723	1,067
2002	732	421	617	731	1,090
2003	744	429	628	740	1,131
2004	762	446	645	761	1,143
2005	771	455	652	766	1,167
2006	797	469	678	796	1,205
2007	823	481	689	810	1,243
2008	857	497	709	830	1,285
2009	873	500	716	835	1,327
2010	874	486	710	845	1,330
2011	886	488	720	840	1,332

NOTE: The comparability of historical labor force data has been affected at various times by methodological and other changes in the Current Population Survey (CPS). Information about historical comparability is online at **www.bls.gov/cps/documentation.htm#comp.**

SOURCE: U.S. Bureau of Labor Statistics.

Table 26. **Median hourly earnings of wage and salary workers paid hourly rates, in current dollars, by sex and age, 1979–2011 annual averages**

Year and sex	Total, 16 years and older	16 to 24 years			25 years and older					
		Total	16 to 19 years	20 to 24 years	Total	25 to 34 years	35 to 44 years	45 to 54 years	55 to 64 years	65 years and older
Both Sexes										
1979................	$4.44	$3.49	$3.10	$4.02	$5.11	$5.20	$5.29	$5.16	$4.97	$3.23
1980................	4.82	3.71	3.22	4.29	5.55	5.66	5.76	5.65	5.39	3.56
1981................	5.15	3.97	3.58	4.61	5.99	6.09	6.20	6.01	5.81	3.92
1982................	5.40	4.05	3.60	4.66	6.28	6.35	6.61	6.42	6.11	4.12
1983................	5.59	4.08	3.61	4.69	6.55	6.50	6.91	6.73	6.41	4.40
1984................	5.83	4.18	3.65	4.82	6.84	6.77	7.17	7.08	6.62	4.63
1985................	6.03	4.26	3.67	4.94	7.05	6.92	7.49	7.37	6.91	4.74
1986................	6.20	4.41	3.71	5.06	7.23	7.01	7.79	7.73	7.17	4.97
1987................	6.47	4.59	3.81	5.21	7.46	7.19	7.94	7.86	7.42	5.08
1988................	6.73	4.79	4.03	5.38	7.74	7.43	8.17	8.16	7.48	5.23
1989................	6.99	4.95	4.22	5.65	7.94	7.64	8.56	8.42	7.82	5.42
1990................	7.23	5.16	4.49	5.91	8.16	7.90	8.82	8.79	8.02	5.75
1991................	7.50	5.26	4.69	6.00	8.48	8.04	9.17	9.11	8.19	5.94
1992................	7.72	5.37	4.73	6.03	8.73	8.17	9.38	9.52	8.48	6.14
1993................	7.87	5.51	4.80	6.15	8.95	8.27	9.61	9.86	8.90	6.39
1994................	8.01	5.62	4.91	6.22	9.12	8.38	9.92	10.02	9.02	6.39
1995................	8.17	5.80	5.04	6.42	9.36	8.71	10.02	10.13	9.20	6.65
1996................	8.40	5.94	5.17	6.69	9.62	8.82	10.14	10.24	9.39	6.77
1997................	8.75	6.15	5.51	6.91	9.87	9.04	10.36	10.60	9.73	6.89
1998................	9.10	6.58	5.88	7.24	10.13	9.65	10.86	10.96	10.08	7.40
1999................	9.53	6.87	6.08	7.74	10.47	9.98	11.02	11.33	10.38	7.70
2000................	9.91	7.24	6.41	8.07	10.88	10.18	11.35	11.82	10.82	8.05
2001................	10.19	7.69	6.76	8.38	11.40	10.67	11.97	12.17	11.37	8.53
2002................	10.47	7.81	6.91	8.47	11.83	10.98	12.18	12.46	11.85	9.07
2003................	10.85	7.90	6.93	8.66	12.05	11.25	12.46	12.97	12.19	9.19
2004................	11.00	7.98	7.00	8.78	12.23	11.37	12.89	13.23	12.58	9.62
2005................	11.19	8.07	7.05	8.91	12.48	11.76	13.11	13.48	12.95	9.93
2006................	11.76	8.24	7.23	9.16	12.94	11.95	13.49	14.03	13.33	10.15
2007................	11.95	8.65	7.57	9.66	13.16	12.05	13.93	14.39	13.71	10.37
2008................	12.23	8.87	7.84	9.76	13.81	12.50	14.38	14.87	14.20	10.89
2009................	12.44	8.90	7.92	9.77	13.91	12.60	14.59	14.85	14.70	11.49
2010................	12.50	8.90	8.00	9.53	13.98	12.53	14.61	14.98	14.89	11.55
2011................	12.71	8.97	8.06	9.61	14.12	12.71	14.83	15.00	15.07	12.19

See note at end of table.

Table 26. **Median hourly earnings of wage and salary workers paid hourly rates, in current dollars, by sex and age, 1979–2011 annual averages—cont'd**

Year and sex	Total, 16 years and older	16 to 24 years			25 years and older					
		Total	16 to 19 years	20 to 24 years	Total	25 to 34 years	35 to 44 years	45 to 54 years	55 to 64 years	65 years and older
Women										
1979	$3.62	$3.19	$3.03	$3.52	$3.90	$4.04	$3.97	$3.84	$3.75	$3.12
1980	3.95	3.45	3.14	3.79	4.24	4.44	4.29	4.23	4.08	3.38
1981	4.28	3.71	3.52	4.09	4.69	4.89	4.77	4.59	4.43	3.71
1982	4.61	3.78	3.55	4.19	5.02	5.19	5.08	4.95	4.80	3.93
1983	4.80	3.82	3.55	4.26	5.23	5.44	5.31	5.19	5.07	4.16
1984	4.97	3.93	3.59	4.36	5.48	5.60	5.61	5.51	5.27	4.37
1985	5.13	4.01	3.61	4.56	5.73	5.79	5.91	5.76	5.46	4.43
1986	5.33	4.11	3.65	4.71	5.95	5.95	6.13	5.99	5.75	4.73
1987	5.60	4.22	3.71	4.89	6.16	6.14	6.35	6.28	6.03	4.85
1988	5.84	4.48	3.91	5.05	6.44	6.36	6.76	6.59	6.08	5.12
1989	6.11	4.69	4.10	5.23	6.78	6.68	7.10	6.90	6.38	5.14
1990	6.44	4.95	4.35	5.57	7.07	7.01	7.37	7.16	6.73	5.45
1991	6.75	5.08	4.64	5.71	7.34	7.19	7.73	7.61	6.95	5.76
1992	6.96	5.16	4.69	5.77	7.65	7.45	7.99	7.94	7.20	5.97
1993	7.12	5.27	4.73	5.96	7.87	7.61	8.16	8.18	7.56	6.18
1994	7.25	5.32	4.83	5.98	8.05	7.78	8.44	8.46	7.82	6.24
1995	7.46	5.49	4.94	6.09	8.17	7.92	8.63	8.72	7.93	6.45
1996	7.73	5.68	5.09	6.26	8.43	8.06	8.89	8.94	8.07	6.45
1997	7.94	5.95	5.42	6.55	8.75	8.20	9.14	9.26	8.31	6.83
1998	8.23	6.24	5.78	6.93	9.13	8.80	9.66	9.78	8.85	7.21
1999	8.64	6.60	5.98	7.22	9.53	9.10	9.83	9.95	9.33	7.50
2000	9.06	7.00	6.23	7.80	9.89	9.69	10.03	10.18	9.84	7.87
2001	9.64	7.25	6.61	8.00	10.20	9.94	10.44	10.85	10.39	8.14
2002	9.89	7.45	6.80	8.11	10.71	10.12	10.98	11.18	10.81	8.73
2003	10.08	7.59	6.85	8.19	11.01	10.51	11.17	11.79	11.05	8.84
2004	10.17	7.71	6.86	8.32	11.23	10.62	11.45	11.95	11.57	9.16
2005	10.31	7.80	6.92	8.50	11.58	10.86	11.84	12.13	11.86	9.82
2006	10.65	7.99	7.11	8.82	11.87	11.07	12.05	12.26	12.12	9.97
2007	10.98	8.15	7.41	9.00	12.05	11.21	12.36	12.85	12.23	10.15
2008	11.49	8.43	7.71	9.16	12.48	11.72	12.89	13.16	13.00	10.53
2009	11.76	8.58	7.82	9.19	12.76	11.96	13.00	13.09	13.59	11.11
2010	11.83	8.62	7.91	9.08	12.88	12.04	13.12	13.50	13.68	11.18
2011	11.98	8.73	7.96	9.16	13.10	12.12	13.44	13.76	14.03	11.76

See note at end of table.

Table 26. Median hourly earnings of wage and salary workers paid hourly rates, in current dollars, by sex and age, 1979–2011 annual averages—cont'd

Year and sex	Total, 16 years and older	16 to 24 years			25 years and older					
		Total	16 to 19 years	20 to 24 years	Total	25 to 34 years	35 to 44 years	45 to 54 years	55 to 64 years	65 years and older
Men										
1979	$5.65	$3.90	$3.19	$4.64	$6.69	$6.38	$7.12	$7.10	$6.59	$3.56
1980	6.10	4.10	3.37	4.92	7.22	6.93	7.81	7.78	7.24	3.79
1981	6.57	4.31	3.64	5.11	7.78	7.33	8.30	8.49	7.88	4.21
1982	6.85	4.38	3.66	5.12	8.08	7.67	8.89	8.88	8.14	4.46
1983	6.92	4.38	3.67	5.05	8.31	7.74	9.22	9.16	8.74	4.75
1984	7.12	4.57	3.72	5.16	8.60	7.88	9.51	9.69	8.86	4.91
1985	7.33	4.68	3.75	5.23	8.85	8.00	9.80	9.97	9.04	4.99
1986	7.59	4.79	3.82	5.43	9.02	8.03	9.99	10.15	9.54	5.18
1987	7.77	4.91	3.95	5.68	9.16	8.26	10.10	10.24	9.72	5.32
1988	7.91	5.03	4.14	5.79	9.38	8.41	10.22	10.69	9.74	5.52
1989	8.10	5.17	4.39	6.02	9.71	8.56	10.59	10.88	10.00	5.90
1990	8.27	5.44	4.64	6.18	9.84	8.83	10.73	11.13	10.17	6.08
1991	8.59	5.58	4.74	6.23	9.98	8.94	10.98	11.71	10.08	6.22
1992	8.67	5.65	4.80	6.24	10.06	9.02	10.93	12.02	10.39	6.45
1993	8.86	5.75	4.87	6.33	10.18	9.10	11.16	12.15	10.96	6.71
1994	9.00	5.88	4.98	6.56	10.29	9.10	11.50	12.10	11.06	6.64
1995	9.23	6.04	5.14	6.82	10.73	9.46	11.89	12.32	11.11	6.85
1996	9.52	6.17	5.25	6.99	10.78	9.70	11.91	12.40	11.15	7.04
1997	9.83	6.45	5.61	7.18	11.10	9.92	12.07	12.80	11.79	6.96
1998	10.06	6.91	5.98	7.78	11.72	10.22	12.48	13.04	12.22	7.74
1999	10.31	7.12	6.18	8.03	12.00	10.84	12.78	13.68	12.21	7.86
2000	10.81	7.63	6.64	8.39	12.24	10.97	13.14	13.90	12.81	8.31
2001	11.32	8.01	6.90	8.92	12.88	11.58	13.92	14.25	12.95	9.00
2002	11.64	8.05	7.02	8.88	13.05	11.89	13.96	14.40	13.38	9.78
2003	11.89	8.14	7.02	9.00	13.25	12.01	14.13	14.93	14.09	9.79
2004	12.02	8.21	7.15	9.07	13.74	12.03	14.60	15.11	14.54	9.90
2005	12.16	8.42	7.21	9.20	13.91	12.17	14.88	15.13	14.79	10.04
2006	12.68	8.79	7.43	9.75	14.27	12.63	15.06	16.04	15.04	10.72
2007	12.95	9.13	7.77	9.96	14.75	12.83	15.17	16.15	15.45	11.01
2008	13.46	9.24	7.98	10.00	15.03	13.47	16.02	16.82	15.90	11.50
2009	13.76	9.22	8.05	9.99	15.07	13.20	16.10	16.99	16.09	12.00
2010	13.76	9.21	8.09	9.90	15.04	13.10	15.83	16.89	16.45	11.92
2011	13.80	9.23	8.16	9.90	15.11	13.18	16.03	16.88	17.07	12.85

NOTE: The comparability of historical labor force data has been affected at various times by methodological and other changes in the Current Population Survey (CPS). Information about historical comparability is online at **www.bls.gov/cps/documentation.htm #comp**.

SOURCE: U.S. Bureau of Labor Statistics.

Table 27. **Median hourly earnings of wage and salary workers paid hourly rates, in current dollars, by sex, race, and Hispanic or Latino ethnicity, 1979–2011 annual averages**

Year and sex	Total, 16 years and older	White	Black or African American	Asian	Hispanic or Latino
Both Sexes					
1979	$4.44	$4.51	$4.11	—	$4.08
1980	4.82	4.88	4.44	—	4.44
1981	5.15	5.18	4.90	—	4.81
1982	5.40	5.47	5.06	—	5.01
1983	5.59	5.66	5.15	—	5.09
1984	5.83	5.90	5.36	—	5.27
1985	6.03	6.10	5.50	—	5.47
1986	6.20	6.28	5.80	—	5.65
1987	6.47	6.56	5.99	—	5.82
1988	6.73	6.81	6.15	—	5.95
1989	6.99	7.08	6.43	—	6.07
1990	7.23	7.33	6.81	—	6.28
1991	7.50	7.61	7.00	—	6.46
1992	7.72	7.82	7.06	—	6.65
1993	7.87	7.97	7.18	—	6.83
1994	8.01	8.11	7.29	—	6.93
1995	8.17	8.32	7.66	—	7.00
1996	8.40	8.57	7.76	—	7.17
1997	8.75	8.88	8.01	—	7.39
1998	9.10	9.22	8.39	—	7.92
1999	9.53	9.74	8.85	—	8.07
2000	9.91	9.96	9.34	$10.07	8.54
2001	10.19	10.26	9.73	10.75	9.06
2002	10.47	10.71	9.93	10.36	9.22
2003	10.85	10.97	10.15	11.12	9.76
2004	11.00	11.13	10.19	11.10	9.81
2005	11.19	11.48	10.17	12.01	9.95
2006	11.76	11.86	10.63	12.53	10.12
2007	11.95	12.08	10.89	12.22	10.24
2008	12.23	12.54	11.20	13.01	10.97
2009	12.44	12.66	11.64	13.16	11.04
2010	12.50	12.74	11.77	13.22	10.88
2011	12.71	12.91	11.79	13.35	11.05

See note at end of table.

Table 27. **Median hourly earnings of wage and salary workers paid hourly rates, in current dollars, by sex, race, and Hispanic or Latino ethnicity, 1979–2011 annual averages—cont'd**

Year and sex	Total, 16 years and older	White	Black or African American	Asian	Hispanic or Latino
Women					
1979	$3.62	$3.62	$3.55	—	$3.44
1980	3.95	3.96	3.88	—	3.78
1981	4.28	4.28	4.19	—	4.10
1982	4.61	4.61	4.49	—	4.33
1983	4.80	4.81	4.72	—	4.42
1984	4.97	4.98	4.87	—	4.65
1985	5.13	5.14	5.04	—	4.82
1986	5.33	5.35	5.17	—	5.00
1987	5.60	5.62	5.40	—	5.11
1988	5.84	5.86	5.61	—	5.28
1989	6.11	6.13	5.88	—	5.53
1990	6.44	6.46	6.23	—	5.80
1991	6.75	6.76	6.55	—	5.98
1992	6.96	6.99	6.64	—	6.17
1993	7.12	7.16	6.87	—	6.31
1994	7.25	7.34	6.93	—	6.40
1995	7.46	7.54	7.12	—	6.60
1996	7.73	7.79	7.20	—	6.77
1997	7.94	8.00	7.59	—	6.82
1998	8.23	8.33	7.90	—	7.22
1999	8.64	8.73	8.13	—	7.46
2000	9.06	9.09	8.86	$9.77	7.89
2001	9.64	9.73	9.15	10.07	8.28
2002	9.89	9.94	9.45	10.10	8.54
2003	10.08	10.11	9.91	10.68	8.88
2004	10.17	10.21	9.93	10.57	9.04
2005	10.31	10.50	9.93	11.64	9.18
2006	10.65	10.77	10.11	11.95	9.50
2007	10.98	11.06	10.45	11.83	9.80
2008	11.49	11.70	10.78	12.25	10.07
2009	11.76	11.83	11.01	12.67	10.09
2010	11.83	11.88	11.20	12.41	10.11
2011	11.98	12.05	11.28	12.80	10.25

See note at end of table.

Table 27. **Median hourly earnings of wage and salary workers paid hourly rates, in current dollars, by sex, race, and Hispanic or Latino ethnicity, 1979–2011 annual averages—cont'd**

Year and sex	Total, 16 years and older	White	Black or African American	Asian	Hispanic or Latino
Men					
1979	$5.65	$5.79	$4.83	—	$4.79
1980	6.10	6.23	5.13	—	5.03
1981	6.57	6.71	5.81	—	5.37
1982	6.85	6.98	5.97	—	5.73
1983	6.92	7.07	5.96	—	5.81
1984	7.12	7.26	6.13	—	6.04
1985	7.33	7.58	6.15	—	6.07
1986	7.59	7.78	6.57	—	6.19
1987	7.77	7.93	6.74	—	6.37
1988	7.91	8.06	6.94	—	6.51
1989	8.10	8.28	7.07	—	6.66
1990	8.27	8.55	7.37	—	6.74
1991	8.59	8.82	7.57	—	6.88
1992	8.67	8.89	7.62	—	6.99
1993	8.86	9.07	7.67	—	7.12
1994	9.00	9.21	7.92	—	7.17
1995	9.23	9.62	8.16	—	7.26
1996	9.52	9.79	8.18	—	7.62
1997	9.83	9.96	8.67	—	7.90
1998	10.06	10.18	9.09	—	8.24
1999	10.31	10.61	9.77	—	8.61
2000	10.81	10.95	9.98	$10.79	9.04
2001	11.32	11.61	10.18	11.84	9.67
2002	11.64	11.86	10.24	11.02	9.92
2003	11.89	12.03	10.81	11.89	10.03
2004	12.02	12.16	10.88	11.90	10.02
2005	12.16	12.47	10.90	12.75	10.19
2006	12.68	12.88	11.42	13.18	10.84
2007	12.95	13.22	11.57	13.22	11.07
2008	13.46	13.85	11.99	14.03	11.83
2009	13.76	13.95	12.27	14.01	11.92
2010	13.76	13.97	12.16	14.11	11.73
2011	13.80	14.02	12.06	14.25	11.81

NOTE: The comparability of historical labor force data has been affected at various times by methodological and other changes in the Current Population Survey (CPS). Information about historical comparability is online at **www.bls.gov/cps/documentation.htm#comp**. As of 2003, estimates for the race groups listed (White, Black or African American, and Asian) include persons who selected that race group only; persons who selected more than one race group are not included. Prior to 2003, persons who reported more than one race were included in the group they identified as the main race. Persons whose ethnicity is identified as Hispanic or Latino may be of any race. Asian data for 2000–2002 are for Asians and Pacific Islanders. As of 2003, Asians constitute a separate category. Data for Asians were not tabulated prior to 2000.

Dash indicates data not available.

SOURCE: U.S. Bureau of Labor Statistics.

Technical Note

The estimates in this report were obtained from the Current Population Survey (CPS), which provides a wide range of information on the labor force, employment, and unemployment. The survey is conducted monthly for the U.S. Bureau of Labor Statistics (BLS) by the U.S. Census Bureau, using a national sample of about 60,000 households, with coverage in all 50 states and the District of Columbia. The earnings data are collected from one-fourth of the CPS monthly sample.

Material in this report is in the public domain and may be used without permission. This information is available to sensory-impaired individuals upon request. Voice telephone: (202) 691-5200; Federal Relay Service: 1 (800) 877-8339.

Concepts and definitions

The principal concepts and definitions used in connection with the earnings data in this report are described next.

Usual weekly earnings. Data are collected on wages and salaries before taxes and other deductions, and include any overtime pay, commissions, and tips usually received (at the principal job in the case of multiple jobholders). All self-employed workers are excluded, both those with incorporated businesses and those with unincorporated businesses. Prior to 1994, respondents were asked how much they usually earned per week. Since January 1994, respondents have been asked to identify the easiest way for them to report earnings (hourly, weekly, biweekly, twice monthly, monthly, annually, or other) and how much they usually earn in the period reported. Earnings reported on a basis other than weekly are converted to a weekly equivalent. The term "usual" is as perceived by the respondent. If the respondent asks for a definition of "usual," interviewers are instructed to define the term as "more than half the weeks worked during the past 4 or 5 months."

Medians (and other quantiles) of weekly earnings. Most of the earnings estimates shown in this report are medians. The median (or upper limit of the second quartile) is the amount that divides a given earnings distribution into two equal groups, one having earnings above the median and the other having earnings below the median. Ten percent of workers in a given distribution have earnings below the upper limit of the first decile (90 percent have higher earnings), 25 percent have earnings below the upper limit of the first quartile (75 percent have higher earnings), 75 percent have earnings below the upper limit of the third quartile (25 percent have higher earnings), and 90 percent have earnings below the upper limit of the ninth decile (10 percent have higher earnings).

The BLS estimating procedure for determining the median of an earnings distribution places each reported or calculated weekly earnings value into a $50-wide interval that is centered around a multiple of $50. The median is estimated through the linear interpolation of the interval in which the median lies.

Over-the-year changes in the medians (and other quantile boundaries) for specific groups may not necessarily be consistent with the movements estimated for the overall quantile boundary. The most common reasons for this possible anomaly are as follows:

- There could be a change in the relative weights of the subgroups. For example, the medians of both 16- to 24-year-olds and those 25 years and older may rise, but if the lower earning 16-to-24 age group accounts for a greatly increased share of the total, the overall median could actually fall.

- There could be a large change in the shape of the distribution of reported earnings, particularly near a quantile boundary. This change could be caused by survey observations that are clustered at rounded values—for example, $300, $400, or $500. An estimate lying in a $50-wide centered interval containing such a cluster, or "spike," tends to change more slowly than one in other intervals. Consider, for example, the calculation of the median for a multipeaked distribution that shifts over time. As such a distribution shifts, the median does not necessarily move at the same rate. Specifically, the median takes relatively more time to move through a frequently reported earnings interval, but once above the upper limit of such an interval, it can move relatively quickly to the next frequently reported interval. BLS procedures for estimating medians (and other quantile boundaries) mitigate such irregular movements of the measures; however, users should be cautious of these effects when evaluating short-term changes in the medians and in ratios of the medians.

Constant dollars. The Consumer Price Index research series using current methods (CPI-U-RS) is used to convert current dollars to constant dollars. BLS has made numerous improvements to the Consumer Price Index (CPI) over the years. Although these improvements make the CPI more accurate, the official histories of price index series are not adjusted to reflect the improvements. Because many researchers need a historical series that measures price change consistently over time, BLS developed the CPI-U-RS to provide an estimate of the CPI that incorporates most of the methodological improvements made since 1978 into the entire series. (For further information, see Kenneth J. Stewart and Stephen B. Reed, "CPI research series using current methods, 1978–98," *Monthly Labor Review*, June 1999, on the Internet at **www.bls.gov/opub/mlr/1999/06/art4full. pdf**; and "Questions and Answers: Consumer Price Index Research Series Using Current Methods," on the Internet at **www.bls.gov/cpi/cpirsqa.pdf**.)

This report uses the most recent version of the CPI-U-RS available at the time of production. Users should note, however, that the CPI-U-RS is subject to periodic revision. As a result, the rate of inflation incorporated into the constant-dollar earnings estimates in this report may differ from that in previous reports in this series or in other publications.

Wage and salary workers. These are workers who receive wages, salaries, commissions, tips, payment in kind, or piece rates. The group includes employees in both the private and public sectors but, for purposes of the earnings series, excludes all self-employed persons, both those with incorporated businesses and those with unincorporated businesses.

Full-time workers. For the purpose of producing estimates of earnings, workers who usually work 35 hours or more per week at their sole or principal job are defined as working full time.

Part-time workers. For the purpose of producing estimates of earnings, workers who usually work less than 35 hours per week at their sole or principal job are defined as working part time.

Workers paid by the hour. Historically, workers paid an hourly wage have made up approximately three-fifths of all wage and salary workers. Workers paid by the hour are included in the full- and part-time worker tables in this report, along with salaried workers and other workers not paid by the hour. Data for workers paid at hourly rates are presented separately in tables 9–12, 21–22, and 26–27.

Workers paid at or below the federal minimum wage. The estimates of the numbers of workers with reported earnings at or below the federal minimum wage in tables 11 and 12 pertain only to workers who are paid hourly rates. Salaried workers and other workers who are not paid by the hour are not included, even though some have earnings that, if converted to hourly rates, would be at or below the minimum wage. Consequently, the estimates presented in this report likely understate the actual number of workers with hourly earnings at or below the minimum wage. Research has shown, however, that the degree of understatement is small. BLS does not routinely estimate the hourly earnings of workers not paid by the hour because of data quality concerns associated with such an estimation process.

The prevailing Federal minimum wage was $2.90, effective January 1, 1979; $3.10, effective January 1, 1980; $3.35, effective January 1, 1981; $3.80, effective April 1, 1990; $4.25, effective April 1, 1991; $4.75, effective October 1, 1996; $5.15, effective September 1, 1997; $5.85, effective July 24, 2007; $6.55, effective July 24, 2008; and $7.25, effective July 24, 2009. Data for 1990–1991, 1996–1997, and 2007–2009 reflect changes in the minimum wage that took place during those years. Note that some states have established minimum-wage standards that exceed the federal level.

The presence of workers with hourly earnings below the minimum wage does not necessarily indicate violations of the Fair Labor Standards Act (FLSA), because there are a number of exemptions to the minimum-wage provisions of the law. In addition, some workers might have rounded their hourly earnings in response to survey questions. As a result, some might have reported hourly earnings below the minimum wage when, in fact, they earned the minimum wage or higher.

Reliability

Statistics based on the CPS are subject to both sampling and nonsampling error. Whenever a sample, rather than an entire population, is surveyed, there is a chance that the sample estimates may differ from the "true" population values they represent. The exact difference, or sampling error, varies with the particular sample selected, and this variability is measured by the standard error of the estimate. There is about a 90-percent chance, or level of confidence, that an estimate based on a sample will differ by no more than 1.6 standard errors from the true population value because of sampling error. BLS analyses generally are conducted at the 90-percent level of confidence. Estimates of earnings and their standard errors can be used to construct approximate confidence intervals, or ranges of values, that include the true population value with known probabilities.

The CPS data also are affected by nonsampling error. This kind of error can occur for many reasons, including the failure to sample a segment of the population, inability to obtain information on all respondents in the sample, inability or unwillingness of respondents to provide correct information, and errors made in data collection or processing. For a full discussion of the reliability of data from the CPS and for information on estimating standard errors, see the "Reliability of the estimates" section of Household Data technical documentation on the Internet at **www.bls.gov/cps/ eetech_methods.pdf.**